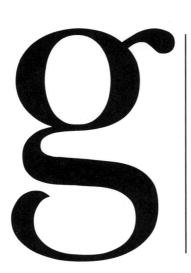

CRITICAL REASONING

Verbal Strategy Guide

This unique guide illustrates how to deconstruct arguments using innovative diagramming techniques designed to build speed and improve accuracy. Understanding the underlying structures of arguments is the key to quick reading and precise analysis.

Critical Reasoning GMAT Strategy Guide, Third Edition

10-digit International Standard Book Number: 0-9818533-0-7
13-digit International Standard Book Number: 978-0-9818533-0-7

8 GUIDE INSTRUCTIONAL SERIES

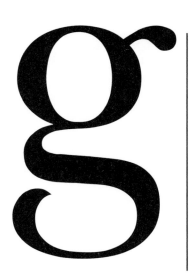

Math GMAT Strategy Guides

Number Properties (ISBN: 978-0-9818533-4-5)

Fractions, Decimals, & Percents (ISBN: 978-0-9818533-2-1)

Equations, Inequalities, & VICs (ISBN: 978-0-9818533-1-4)

Word Translations (ISBN: 978-0-9818533-7-6)

Geometry (ISBN: 978-0-9818533-3-8)

Verbal GMAT Strategy Guides

Critical Reasoning (ISBN: 978-0-9818533-0-7)

Reading Comprehension (ISBN: 978-0-9818533-5-2)

Sentence Correction (ISBN: 978-0-9818533-6-9)

ManhattanGMAT
the new standard

September 30th, 2008

Dear Student,

Thank you for picking up one of the Manhattan GMAT Strategy Guides—we hope that this book makes it easier for you to read, understand, and solve Critical Reasoning questions.

As with most accomplishments, there were many people involved in the various iterations of the book that you're holding. First and foremost is Zeke Vanderhoek, the founder of Manhattan GMAT. Zeke was a lone tutor in New York when he started the Company in 2000. Now, eight years later, MGMAT has Instructors and offices nationwide, and the Company contributes to the studies and successes of thousands of students each year.

These 3rd Edition Strategy Guides have been refashioned and honed based upon the continuing experiences of our Instructors and our students. We owe much of these latest editions to the insight provided by our students. On the Company side, we are indebted to many of our Instructors, including but not limited to Josh Braslow, Dan Gonzalez, Mike Kim, Stacey Koprince, Jadran Lee, Ron Purewal, Tate Shafer, Emily Sledge, and of course Chris Ryan, the Company's Lead Instructor and Director of Curriculum Development.

At Manhattan GMAT, we continually aspire to provide the best Instructors and resources possible. We hope that you'll find our dedication manifest in this book. If you have any comments or questions, please e-mail me at andrew.yang@manhattangmat.com. I'll be sure that your comments reach Chris and the rest of the team—and I'll read them too.

Best of luck in preparing for the GMAT!

Sincerely,

Andrew Yang
Chief Executive Officer
Manhattan GMAT

HOW TO ACCESS YOUR ONLINE RESOURCES

Please read this entire page of information, all the way down to the bottom of the page! This page describes WHAT online resources are included with the purchase of this book and HOW to access these resources.

If you are a registered Manhattan GMAT student and have received this book as part of your course materials, you have AUTOMATIC access to ALL of our online resources. This includes all practice exams, question banks, and online updates to this book. To access these resources, follow the instructions in the Welcome Guide provided to you at the start of your program. Do NOT follow the instructions below.

If you have purchased this book, your purchase includes 1 YEAR OF ONLINE ACCESS to the following:

> **6 Computer Adaptive Online Practice Exams**
>
> **Bonus Online Question Bank for *CRITICAL REASONING***
>
> **Online Updates to the Content in this Book**

The 6 full-length computer adaptive practice exams included with the purchase of this book are delivered online using Manhattan GMAT's proprietary computer-adaptive test engine. The exams adapt to your ability level by drawing from a bank of more than 1,200 unique questions of varying difficulty levels written by Manhattan GMAT's expert instructors, all of whom have scored in the 99th percentile on the Official GMAT. At the end of each exam you will receive a score, an analysis of your results, and the opportunity to review detailed explanations for each question. You may choose to take the exams timed or untimed.

The Bonus Online Question Bank for *CRITICAL REASONING* consists of 25 extra practice questions (with detailed explanations) that test the variety of Critical Reasoning concepts and skills covered in this book. These questions provide you with extra practice *beyond* the problem sets contained in this book. You may use our online timer to practice your pacing by setting time limits for each question in the bank.

The content presented in this book is updated periodically to ensure that it reflects the GMAT's most current trends. You may view all updates, including any known errors or changes, upon registering for online access.

Important Note: The 6 computer adaptive online exams included with the purchase of this book are the SAME exams that you receive upon purchasing ANY book in Manhattan GMAT's 8 Book Strategy Series. On the other hand, the Bonus Online Question Bank for *CRITICAL REASONING* is a unique resource that you receive ONLY with the purchase of this specific title.

To access the online resources listed above, you will need this book in front of you and you will need to register your information online. This book includes access to the above resources for ONE PERSON ONLY.

To register and start using your online resources, please go online to the following URL:

http://www.manhattangmat.com/access.cfm   (Double check that you have typed this in accurately!)

Your one year of online access begins on the day that you register at the above URL. You only need to register your product ONCE at the above URL. To use your online resources any time AFTER you have completed the registration process, please login to the following URL:

http://www.manhattangmat.com/practicecenter.cfm

TABLE OF CONTENTS

g

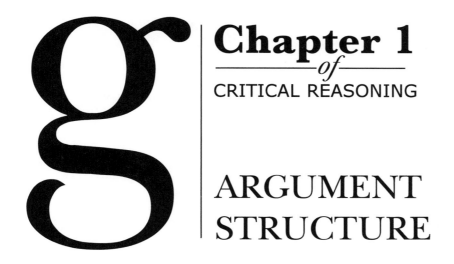

Chapter 1
of
CRITICAL REASONING

ARGUMENT STRUCTURE

In This Chapter . . .

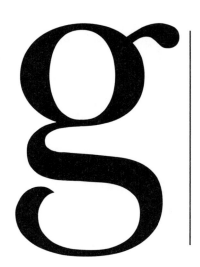

- Identifying the Parts of an Argument
- Finding the Conclusion
- Common Signal Words for Argument Parts
- An Alternate Way to Find the Conclusion

ARGUMENT STRUCTURE

Critical Reasoning questions on the GMAT involve reading brief arguments (each argument is generally one to three sentences long) and answering questions relating to those arguments.

In order to analyze GMAT arguments, it is important to understand their basic structure:

Premises + (Assumptions) = Conclusion

In words, premises and assumptions lead to a conclusion.

PREMISES are STATED pieces of information or evidence that generally provide support for the given conclusion. They may be facts, opinions, or claims. If they are opinions or claims, they will not be the overall claim the author is making; rather, they will be some intermediate claim the author is using to support the overall claim (or conclusion).

ASSUMPTIONS are UNSTATED parts of the argument that are NECESSARY to reach the given conclusion. In the formula above, the word **Assumptions** is put in parentheses to signal that assumptions are NEVER stated in the written argument.

The main point of the argument is the CONCLUSION, which is logically supported by the assumptions and premises. Conclusions are in the form of an opinion or a claim.

You can think of the conclusion of an argument as the top of a building, supported by the building itself (the premises) and the unseen underground foundation (the assumptions).

Premises present facts or claims that usually support the conclusion of the argument.

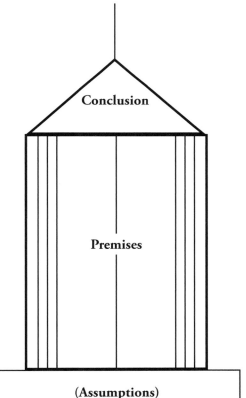

Identifying the Parts of an Argument

In order to do well on GMAT Critical Reasoning questions, you must be able to identify the parts of an argument quickly. Consider the following argument:

> Studying regularly is one factor that has been shown to improve one's performance on the GMAT. Melissa took the GMAT and scored a 500. If she studies several times a week, Melissa can expect to improve her score.

In analyzing an argument, **you should first look for the conclusion**, which is the main point of the argument. The conclusion is often the last sentence of an argument, but not always. Sometimes the conclusion appears as the first sentence.

Where is the CONCLUSION? The main point of this argument is the last sentence:

> If she studies several times a week, Melissa can expect to improve her score.

After finding the conclusion, look for the premises that lead to the conclusion. Premises include ALL the pieces of information written in the argument (except the conclusion). Premises provide evidence that usually supports, or leads to, the conclusion.

Where are the PREMISES? Since everything except the conclusion is considered a premise, each of the first two sentences is a premise.

> Premise: Studying regularly is one factor that has been shown to improve one's performance on the GMAT.
> Premise: Melissa took the GMAT and scored a 500.

Often, all you will need to find are the conclusion and the premises. Sometimes, however, the GMAT will ask you to identify an assumption.

Where are the ASSUMPTIONS? Assumptions are unstated parts of the argument. Therefore, you will NEVER find an assumption stated in an argument. However, assumptions are NECESSARY to reach the given conclusion. For example, one assumption in this argument is that studying several times a week qualifies as studying regularly.

The conclusion comes last logically, but does not necessarily appear last in the text of the argument.

Finding the Conclusion

Arguments on the GMAT are generally written so that the conclusion is fairly easy to identify. Most of the time, the conclusion is presented in one of three common ways. Since two of these ways involve the question, **you should read the question first when you approach any new Critical Reasoning problem.**

Type A: <u>Question contains the conclusion.</u>

> Some universities are changing the structure of financial aid awards given to students who cannot afford to pay full tuition. In the past, the largest proportion of financial aid distributed to students was in the form of federal, interest-deferred loans. Now, these institutions are awarding a higher proportion of grants, money that students do not need to pay back.
>
> If, on the basis of the evidence above, it is argued that the shift from loan to grant awards gives students the freedom to choose careers in less lucrative professions, which of the following, if true, would most seriously weaken that argument?

The CONCLUSION of this argument is given in the question: The shift from loan to grant awards gives students the freedom to choose careers in less lucrative professions. This assertion is the main point of the argument. (The question goes on to ask for a way to weaken the argument. We will discuss how to address this kind of question later in this guide.)

Type B: <u>Question hints at the conclusion in the argument.</u>

> A program instituted by a state government to raise money allows homeowners to prepay their future property taxes at the current rate. Even if the government were to raise the tax rate in a subsequent year, any prepaid taxes would allow the homeowner to maintain taxes at the lower rate, lowering the overall property tax burden over time. For this reason, homeowners should participate in the program.
>
> Which of the following is an assumption that supports the indicated rationale for homeowners participating in the program?

The CONCLUSION of this argument is hinted at in the question. The word *rationale* points us to the final sentence: For this reason, homeowners should participate in the program. *Reason* and *rationale* are synonyms.

Incidentally, the reason is located in the sentence prior to the conclusion: any prepaid taxes would allow the homeowner to maintain taxes at the lower rate, lowering the overall property tax burden over time. In essence, the question is asking us to determine an assumption that connects this premise and the argument's conclusion.

Most GMAT arguments provide clues about the location of the conclusion via keywords in the argument or in the question itself.

Manhattan **GMAT*** Prep
the new standard

Type C: <u>Argument contains an obvious conclusion.</u>

> Transportation safety data indicate that trains are safer than cars, and that airplanes are safer than trains. Injuries and deaths per passenger-mile of airplane travel are less than one-tenth the figure for car travel. Therefore, buses must also be more dangerous than airplanes.
>
> Which of the following, if true, most significantly weakens the argument?

The question contains no specific reference to any information in the argument. In this case, for the majority of questions, the argument will contain a very clear signal word or expression that indicates the conclusion. In this case, the signal is the word *Therefore* at the beginning of the third sentence.

Which type is this example?

> Certain genetic diseases are more prevalent among certain ethnic populations. For example, Tay Sachs disease, a usually fatal genetic condition caused by the build-up of gangliocides in nerve cells, occurs more frequently among Ashkenazi Jews than among the general population.
>
> Which of the following assertions can most properly be drawn from the above information?

Where is the conclusion? The question does not contain any clues; neither does the body of the argument.

In fact, the argument above does not contain a conclusion at all; both sentences present <u>factual information</u> rather than a claim. Some GMAT Critical Reasoning questions ask *you* to draw a conclusion, make an inference, or explain a situation using only a passage of premises. In these cases, the conclusion will be in the <u>answer choices</u> (though, as you will see in the "Draw a Conclusion" chapter, the correct conclusion will not look very much like the kinds of conclusions that other GMAT arguments usually present).

Read the question first to determine the conclusion efficiently.

Common Signal Words for Argument Parts

As we discussed earlier, the conclusion of an argument is often preceded by certain signal words. You should be on the lookout for these conclusion signals:

Therefore	**So**
As a result	**Consequently**
Suggests	**Thus**
Indicates	**Hence**
Accordingly	**It follows that**

Conclusions can also be signaled by their strong tone, often marked by "opinion" words such as **should** ("This law **should** be enacted…").

Likewise, certain other words signal premises. Here are the most common premise signals:

Since	**Because**
Due to	**Given that**
As a result of	**As**

An Alternate Way To Find the Conclusion

This section discusses what to do when the primary patterns for finding the conclusion do not apply.

As we discussed earlier, the primary patterns will appear the vast majority of the time. On a few minor and/or more difficult questions, however, we may need to work a little bit harder to find the conclusion.

You should not use this method unless the primary patterns do not apply, as this alternate method is more difficult and could lead you to the wrong conclusion.

First: Identify All Claims

In order to separate the conclusion from the premises, first identify all claims made in the argument. You should distinguish claims from facts, which can be proven true. Claims often contain one or more of the following three types of language:

A. *Predict the Future.* Look out for verbs or verb constructions that are in the future tense or that otherwise refer to the future. For example:

will, should, can be expected to, could result in, are likely to, etc.

Most statements that take place in the future are claims. For example:

- If she studies several times a week, Melissa **can expect to** improve her score.

- Homeowners **should** participate in the program in order to decrease their overall property tax burden over time.

> When the conclusion is not obvious, first identify all claims, then determine which claim follows logically from all the others.

B. *Subjective Opinion.* Anything that expresses an opinion is likely to be a claim. Similarly, anything that cannot be proven, only argued, is likely to be a claim. For example:

- The proposal to hire additional dogcatchers in Newtown is a mistake.

- Ballroom dancing is more of an art form than a sport.

- The mayor's plan is likely to fail.

C. *Cause and Effect.* Cause and effect statements are signaled by a number of key words:

- **If** X happens, **then** Y happens.

- **As a result of** *or* **because of** *or* **since** X, Y will happen.

- X happens, **so** Y will result.

> A statement that **predicts the future, offers an opinion,** or **posits a cause and effect relationship** is a good candidate for the conclusion of the argument.

If you find only one claim, you are done—that is the conclusion! If you find more than one, move on to the second step.

Second: Use the "Therefore" Test

The conclusion of the argument is the FINAL claim. In other words, every other claim leads to the conclusion, which is <u>logically last in the sequence of events</u>.

If you have two claims, X and Y, ask yourself: Does X lead to Y? Or does Y lead to X? To apply the "Therefore" test, try saying the claims two ways:

(1) "X, **therefore** Y."   If this works, Y is the conclusion.

(2) "Y, **therefore** X."   If this works, X is the conclusion.

For example:

> Manager: the new manufacturing process should save us time in the end, even though the first step of the five-step process will take twice as long as it does under the old process. Far fewer of the components will be found defective and the sole purpose of steps two and three under the old process is to weed out defective components. As a result, we should be able to eliminate two of the five steps in the existing manufacturing process.

> Which of the following would be most useful in evaluating the claim made in the argument?

The question does not tell us what we should focus on as the conclusion. We have two major claims in this argument:

X: *The new process should save us time.*
Y: *We should be able to eliminate two of the five steps in the process.*

So we have two options: X, therefore Y. Or Y, therefore X.

X, therefore Y: *The new process should save us time;* ***therefore****, we should be able to eliminate two of the five steps in the process.*

Y, therefore X: *We should be able to eliminate two of the five steps in the process;* ***therefore****, the new process should save us time.*

Which way is right? In this case, Y leads us to X: <u>first</u> we need to eliminate two of the five steps, and <u>then</u>, <u>as a result</u> of that elimination, the new process saves time.

X is the final claim in the logical chain of events, so X is the conclusion. The deduction that takes place last *logically (or chronologically) in the sequence of events* is the conclusion. Note that the conclusion will not necessarily appear in the last sentence of the argument.

Also, notice that you could have been distracted by a signal expression in front of claim Y: *As a result.* These words tell you that the claim Y is a result of something else (in this case, other premises). But you should not assume that claim Y is the conclusion; in fact, it leads to another, even bigger claim (which <u>is</u> the conclusion).

To test the logical relationship of two claims, you can use other connectors besides *therefore.* Other words or expressions that work the same way include *so, thus,* and *as a result.* Any of these expressions can signal the conclusion.

Remember that you should only use the "Therefore" test if the question does not tell you what the conclusion is or does not give you keywords from the argument that point to the conclusion. If the question does provide such information, that information trumps the "therefore" test.

If the primary ways to find the conclusion do not work, use the "Therefore" test.

Problem Set

Now that you have completed your study of ARGUMENT STRUCTURE, it is time to test your skills on a variety of different arguments. The passages below exhibit a representative sampling of argument structures. For each argument, complete the following in a notebook:

(1) Find and write out the conclusion of the argument. The conclusion may be an entire sentence or part of a sentence. Try to be as accurate as possible in locating the exact words of the conclusion. Indicate how you found the conclusion:

(A) The question contains the conclusion.

(B) The question hints at the conclusion in the argument.

(C) The argument contains an obvious conclusion.

(D) An alternate method (for instance, you identified the claims and if necessary used the "Therefore" test).

(2) If the argument does not include a conclusion, indicate this with the words **no given conclusion**.

Note that you are not actually answering these questions! You are only identifying the conclusion of each argument. During the actual exam, of course, you will not have time to consider which strategy you are using or which type of argument you are facing—at that point, these ideas should be second nature to you. Finding conclusions is a skill that *must* be mastered in order to succeed in answering Critical Reasoning questions accurately. After you are done with the entire set, you may check your work using the answers that follow.

1. The Chinese white dolphin is a territorial animal that rarely strays far from its habitat in the Pearl River Delta. In recent years, increasing industrial and agricultural runoff to the Delta's waters has caused many white dolphins to perish before they reach breeding age. Unless legislation is enacted to ensure there is no further decline in the Delta's water quality, the Chinese white dolphin will become extinct.

    Which of the following, if true, undermines the claim that the Chinese white dolphin will disappear without legislation to preserve water quality in the Delta?

2. A series of research studies has reported that flaxseed oil can have a beneficial effect in reducing tumor growth in mice, particularly the kind of tumor found in human postmenopausal breast cancer. Thus, flaxseed oil should be recommended as an addition to the diets of all postmenopausal women.

    Which of the following is an assumption upon which the argument depends?

3. Violent video games are periodically criticized by some parents' groups, psychologists, religious organizations, and politicians. A common focus of the criticism is that video games that allow players to act out crimes, and reward players for doing so, encourage aggressive behavior. Though some psychological studies have shown a correlation between the playing of violent video games and aggressive behavior, the vast majority of such studies do not claim behavioral causation.

   Which of the following assertions can most properly be drawn from the given information?

4. The source of Pure Springs bottled water is an aquifer hundreds of feet below the surface of the Earth. Because this aquifer contains fewer contaminants and less bacteria than any other domestic aquifer, a spokesperson for Pure Springs claims that the company produces the best tasting bottled water currently available.

   Which of the following, if true, provides the best support for the company spokesperson's claim?

5. Most doctors recommend drinking alcohol in moderation, since the excessive intake of alcohol has been linked to several diseases of the liver. Last year, however, more non-drinkers than drinkers were diagnosed with liver failure. Thus, at least concerning the liver, it can be concluded that drinking alcohol is no more dangerous than abstaining from alcohol.

   Which of the following, if true, most seriously weakens the argument?

6. During the past thirty years, the percentage of the population that smokes cigarettes has consistently declined. During the same time period, however, the number of lung cancer deaths attributed to smoking cigarettes has increased.

   Which of the following can be most properly inferred from the passage?

7. The cutback in physical education is the primary contributing factor to North High School's increasing failure rate on the high school graduation examination. Last year, when students participated in gym class on a daily basis, 85 percent of the school's seniors passed the exam. This year, students have gym class twice weekly, and only 70 percent of seniors passed the test.

   Which of the following most strongly supports the author's opinion about the primary factor contributing to the observed phenomenon?

8. Food allergies account for more than thirty thousand emergency department visits each year. Often, victims of these episodes are completely unaware of their allergies until they experience a major reaction. Studies show that ninety percent of food allergy reactions are caused by only eight distinct foods. For this reason, individuals should sample a minuscule portion of each of these foods to determine whether a particular food allergy is present.

   The author relies upon which of the following assumptions in drawing the conclusion above?

9. To increase the productivity of the country's workforce, the government should introduce new food guidelines that recommend a vegetarian diet. A study of thousands of men and women revealed that those who stick to a vegetarian diet have IQs that are around five points higher than those who regularly eat meat. The vegetarians were also more likely to have earned advanced degrees and hold high-paying jobs.

   Which of the following, if true, demonstrates that the plan to increase productivity by recommending a vegetarian diet is unlikely to succeed?

10. Editorial: To stem the influx of illegal immigrants, the government is planning to construct a wall along our entire border with Country Y. This wall, however, will do little to actually reduce the number of illegal immigrants. Because few economic opportunities exist in Country Y, individuals will simply develop other creative ways to enter our nation.

    Which of the following is an assumption on which the argument depends?

1. Conclusion type A: the conclusion is given in the question. Third sentence: **Unless legislation is enacted to ensure there is no further decline in the Delta's water quality, the Chinese white dolphin will become extinct.**

2. Conclusion type C: Argument contains obvious conclusion. Second sentence: **Thus, flaxseed oil should be recommended as an addition to the diets of all post-menopausal women.**

3. No conclusion given.

4. Conclusion type B: the question hints at the conclusion. End of second sentence: **Pure Springs claims that the company produces the best tasting bottled water currently available.**

5. Conclusion type C: Argument contains obvious conclusion. Third sentence: **Thus, at least concerning the liver, it can be concluded that drinking alcohol is no more dangerous than abstaining from alcohol.**

6. No conclusion given.

7. Conclusion type B: the question hints at the conclusion. First sentence: **The cutback in physical education is the primary contributing factor to North High School's increasing failure rate on the high school graduation examination.**

8. Conclusion type Alternate: the primary method does not apply, so we have to use the "Therefore" test. End of third sentence: **For this reason, individuals should sample a minuscule portion of each of these foods to determine whether a particular food allergy is present.**

9. Conclusion type A: the conclusion is given in the question. First sentence: **To increase the productivity of the country's workforce, the government should introduce new food guidelines that recommend a vegetarian diet.**

10. Conclusion type Alternate: the primary method does not apply, so we have to use the "Therefore" test. Second sentence: **This wall, however, will do little to actually reduce the number of illegal immigrants.**

Claim #1: **This wall, however, will do little to actually reduce the number of illegal immigrants.**

Claim #2: **individuals will simply develop other creative ways to enter our nation**

Try #1 leading to #2: the wall will not do much to reduce the number of illegal immigrants; therefore, people will find other ways to enter the country.

Also try #2 leading to #1: people will find other ways to enter the country; therefore, the wall will not do much to reduce the number of illegal immigrants.

The second version is correct. In this case, #2 leads to #1.

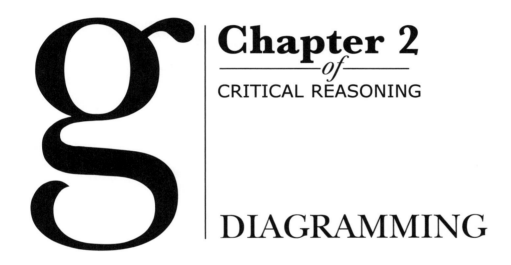

Chapter 2
of
CRITICAL REASONING

DIAGRAMMING

In This Chapter . . .

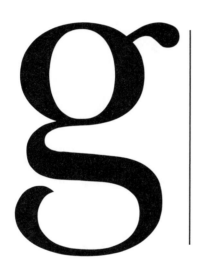

DIAGRAMMING

The most effective way to improve your Critical Reasoning performance on tough problems is to DIAGRAM the argument on paper. The diagramming strategy works for several reasons:

(1) **Diagramming SAVES time:** Critical Reasoning arguments are short but often complex. If you read an argument only once, you may not understand it fully. Rereading the argument several times adds little to comprehension while taking up valuable time. Diagramming an argument makes it readily understandable and saves time spent on repeated readings.

(2) **Diagramming HELPS comprehension:** When you read under pressure, particularly on a test like the GMAT, you may not initially understand what you are reading. The act of diagramming transforms a passive approach into an active process, enabling you to analyze as you read. You will find that you have a much more thorough understanding of the substance of each argument you diagram. This will, in turn, raise your accuracy as you answer Critical Reasoning questions.

> Diagramming can help you save time, improve comprehension and focus on argument structure.

(3) **Diagramming FOCUSES on argument structure:** The questions which the GMAT asks about Critical Reasoning passages are almost always related to one of the structural parts of the argument: the premises, the conclusion, or the hidden assumptions. Diagramming involves identifying and ordering the structural parts of each argument. If you diagram, you can quickly see how each part of the argument relates to the question asked.

How to Diagram an Argument: The T-Diagram

Simply put, diagramming is simply a method of taking summary notes on the argument. Though we offer you one primary technique of diagramming, the form of the diagram is NOT essential. Rather, what matters is the act of analyzing the argument and taking summary notes.

No matter how you diagram, a few principles should guide your work.

(1) **Focus on the essential meaning** when you summarize a point. Omit unnecessary words.

(2) **Use __extreme__ shorthand.** You will only need to use your notes for about 90 seconds. Your short-term memory will naturally retain most of the information, so you can use very brief reminders. For instance, if an argument contrasts small businesses with large businesses, you might write "SB" and "LB." For the next 90 seconds, you will not forget what those abbreviations mean.

This style of note-taking is much more truncated than the style of note-taking you probably developed over years in school. However, on the GMAT, you are not taking notes so that you can study from them later for a quiz. You are taking notes to understand an argument *right now* and answer an exam question within 2 minutes.

(3) **Keep important terms the same.** Avoid changing terms if you can. Feel free to keep the EXACT wording of key points.

(4) **At the same time, make sure you understand what you are writing.** If necessary, rephrase a point slightly as you take notes, so that you grasp the meaning.

The specific method of diagramming that we recommend is called the "T-Diagram."

The T-Diagram

A T-Diagram is visually somewhat like the building analogy we encountered in Chapter 1. The conclusion on top is supported by premises underneath.

First, draw a large T on your scratch paper. Make it asymmetrical, leaving more room on the left side, which will be the "pro" side. In most arguments, you will have very little on the "con" side (on the right).

Step 1.

Second, look for the conclusion. The first place to look for the conclusion is in the question itself. If you do not find it there, then read the argument. Once you find the conclusion, **write it above the top line of the T**, abbreviating heavily.

Step 2.

Conclusion

Third, read or reread the argument sentence by sentence. As you do so, follow the steps below:

- **Write anything that supports the conclusion on the left side of the T** ("Pro" or "Premise for").

- **Write anything that goes against the conclusion on the right side of the T** ("Con" or "Premise against").

- If you find important background information (neither pro nor con), you *might* write that information below the T. Most of the time, however, you will not record such information, since it is usually not critical to solving the problem.

- If you think of something (not in the argument) that might help you to answer the question, you *might* add that information in brackets. For example, if you think of an assumption the author must be making, you could write that at the bottom of your "pro" column. Do not forget the brackets! Otherwise, you might mistake this for an actual premise.

Step 3.

Conclusion
| - Pro | - Con |
| - Pro | |

- *[Assumption]*

Background info

Consider the following example:

> The proposal to hire additional dogcatchers in Newtown is a mistake. Though there is sufficient room in the budget to pay the salaries of the dogcatchers, there are not enough resources available for the town to also pay for the housing and care of the additional canines that the new dogcatchers will be expected to capture.
>
> Which of the following, if true, is the strongest reason to accept the opinion that the proposed plan is a mistake?

The conclusion is in the question. Your T-diagram might look like this:

Plan: hire ↑ dogcatch. = BAD

not suff $ to pay for addl dogs caught	suff $ to pay for ppl

Use the word BUT in your diagram to indicate any changes of direction in the argument.

Diagramming Efficiently

Certain notations can make your diagramming more efficient and effective.

(1) **Abbreviate anything you can**. Remember that you will only need to be able to decipher your notes for about 90 seconds. Turn long words and proper nouns into abbreviations of just two or three letters. Some examples are presented below, but do not limit yourself to these.

Text	Abbreviation
The women's basketball team at State University won the national championship last year	SU W bb won nat chmp last yr
Corporate downsizing led to high unemployment rates and a recession	Corp ↓ → ↑ unemp + recssn
Strategic marketing is necessary to ensure that the money spent provides the greatest possible benefit	Strat mktg = nec: $ for ↑ poss bnft
Quantitative research is more effective than qualitative research	Quant R > Qual R OR Quant R more eff. than Qual R

Do not change or abbreviate so much that you forget or distort the argument. As you develop your diagramming skills, keep in mind that you need to be able to keep <u>all</u> the important details straight as you work on the problems.

(2) **Underline key words and details.** As you summarize each point, underline any words or details that you think may be key to the argument. In particular, you may wish to underline "boundary words," which will be discussed later.

(3) **Use arrows to indicate cause and effect relationships,** which are particularly common.

(4) **Identify point of view with a colon.** If you spot a position or a plan, use a colon to indicate *who* is advocating the position or plan.

Text	T-Diagram
The mayor claims that the fee will reduce congestion	M: fee → ↓ congestion

(5) **Signal any change of direction in the passage with the word BUT in capital letters.** Words that signal a change in direction include *however, despite, but, though, although, surprisingly, still, yet, contrary.* Do not write these out! Just substitute the word BUT.

(6) **Develop your own abbreviations.** Use your own abbreviations and note-taking techniques in addition to those listed above. Practice your techniques and keep them *consistent.*

Some students may benefit from more visually-oriented diagramming approaches that are less text-based and more graphic in nature. You might put dates on a timeline, compare two phenomena in a table, or even draw pictures. It is appropriate to use whatever approach works best for you, as long as you practice it extensively so that you are comfortable using that approach.

Diagramming Model Arguments

Diagramming is a powerful strategy that is best learned by repeated practice with GMAT arguments. It typically takes two to three weeks of frequent practice before a student becomes adept at the technique. The following model diagrams relate to arguments used as examples in Chapter 1. Now, instead of simply analyzing structure, we will actually diagram each argument. Create your own diagram as you read, then compare your diagram to the samples given. Assess whether your diagram captures the argument's essential meaning and structure.

Example 1

Some universities are changing the structure of financial aid awards given to students who cannot afford to pay full tuition. In the past, the largest proportion of financial aid distributed to students was in the form of federal, interest-deferred loans. Now, these institutions are awarding a higher proportion of grants, money that students do not need to pay back.

If, on the basis of the evidence above, it is argued that the shift from loan to grant awards gives students the freedom to choose careers in less lucrative professions, which of the following, if true, would most seriously weaken that argument?

When you diagram, you should not simply transcribe the text! You must simplify as you go.

Read the question first. Notice that it makes an argument (*it is argued that...*). Such language can be a clue that the conclusion is in the question. Put that conclusion at the top of your T. Next, summarize each distinct piece of information as you read it, without reading the whole argument first. Underline any important words. A sample diagram for this argument is provided here:

L → G = stud. can choose ↓ $ jobs

past: <u>mostly</u> loans
        no-int, fed
now: ↑ grants

don't pay back

[Assum: no debt or ↓ debt?]

Notice how much the sample diagram abbreviates the full text of the argument. Also note the optional point in brackets below the T-diagram. This is not information from the argument. Rather, the GMAT test-taker noted down a speculation. As he or she was reading, the following thought occurred to him or her: "The author might be assuming that the switch from loans to grants will reduce or eliminate debt loads for students. Perhaps that is why the author thinks that students will be able to afford to pursue lower-paying jobs." By noting this thought down, the test-taker captures it for later analysis. In fact, since the question asks for a way to weaken the argument, the correct answer choice may attack this assumption.

Putting down your speculations is not necessary and may even be distracting. But if you have an important insight that you think might be key to answering the problem, go ahead and note it down—in brackets.

Example 2

> A program instituted by a state government to raise money allows homeowners to prepay their future property taxes at the current rate. Even if the government were to raise the tax rate in a subsequent year, any prepaid taxes would allow the homeowner to maintain taxes at the lower rate, lowering the overall property tax burden over time. For this reason, homeowners should participate in the program.
>
> Which of the following is an assumption that supports the indicated rationale for homeowners participating in the program?

A good diagram can often expose faulty reasoning in an argument.

DIAGRAMMING STRATEGY

The question contains a hint or "pointer" to the conclusion: the word *rationale*. Scan to find that word or a synonym in the argument. We find the last sentence: *For this reason, homeowners should participate in the program.* This sentence is the conclusion; add it to the top of your T-diagram.

A diagram for this example might appear as follows:

> HO shd do program to prepay txs
> ─────────────────────────────────
> State prog: HO prepay
> prop txs at <u>today's</u> rate
>
> If <u>txs</u> ↑ HO still pays ↓
> rate → save $
>
> [what if txs ↓?]
> [what if move? Rebate?]

Diagrams keep you reading actively. Do not let the words pass through your brain without actually grasping their meaning.

Again, note the significant degree of abbreviation. Your abbreviations may not look like those in the sample diagram. Just make sure that you can decipher your own abbreviations.

Also note the information shown in the brackets below the T-diagram. The test-taker wondered what would happen if taxes went down. Would the homeowner still be locked into the old tax rate, which is now higher than the new one? If that is the case, this plan might not help homeowners. The test-taker also wondered what would happen if the homeowner moved. Would he or she get a rebate for prepaid taxes? If not, then the new plan would be detrimental to homeowners. Either of these speculations could be the basis of a correct assumption that could answer the question.

Example 3

Transportation safety data indicate that trains are safer than cars, and that airplanes are safer than trains. Injuries and deaths per passenger-mile of airplane travel are less than one-tenth the figure for car travel. Therefore, buses must also be more dangerous than airplanes.

Which of the following, if true, most significantly weakens the argument?

Since the question does not reference any specific information in the argument, scan quickly for "conclusion language" in the argument. In this argument, the word *therefore* introduces the third sentence.

An appropriate diagram for this example might appear as follows:

Bus MUST > dang. than pln

safety:
trn > car
pln > trn
per pass-mile:
pln < 1/10 inj/dth as car

[car = bus?]

As you diagram, if you happen to think of assumptions, especially any problematic ones, note them down in brackets at the bottom.

Observe that this diagram includes the question "[car = bus?]." This is a problematic assumption—that buses are comparable to cars—made in the argument and identified by the reader. Noticing problematic assumptions can make answering questions easier.

Example 4

> Certain genetic diseases are more prevalent among certain ethnic populations. For example, Tay Sachs disease, a usually fatal genetic condition caused by the build-up of gangliocides in nerve cells, occurs more frequently among Ashkenazi Jews than among the general population.
>
> Which of the following assertions can most properly be drawn from the above information?

This question contains no information specific to the argument. When you quickly scan the text, no conclusion keywords are apparent. In this case, <u>do not write down anything</u> for the conclusion. Rather, scan the passage point by point, and build your T-diagram. Consider whether any of the points are claims. In this case, the statements are not arguable; indeed, the passage consists entirely of premises. (In addition, the wording of this question indicates that it is a "Draw a Conclusion" question. That is, you will have to find the conclusion in the answer choices. This question type will be discussed in more detail later in Chapter 5.)

Note that the sample diagram, like the argument, contains no conclusion.

> ?
> _____
> some gen. dis. > in
> cert. ethnic pops.
> TS: fatal, gen
>   caused by G in NC(?)
>   > common in AJ

Notice also that, although the second sentence describes how Tay Sachs disease works, this information is represented only very simply in the diagram (and with the addition of a question mark, indicating that the reader did not quite understand that piece of information).

Critical reasoning questions revolve more often around logic, rather than around how some technical fact works, so it is unlikely you would have to understand the phrase **the build-up of gangliocides in nerve cells**. As such, it is not necessary to spend time detailing this sort of technical information. The most you need to understand is that the basic cause for this disease is given. If the question does ask about the cause, then you can take the time to re-read and try to understand that technical phrase.

Problem Set

Now that you have completed your study of diagramming, it is time to test your skills on a variety of different passages. The passages below exhibit a representative sampling of argument structures. These are structured similarly to the passages used in the previous problem set. Diagram each passage in a notebook:

(1) Be sure your diagrams include:
   - One point per line
   - Underlined key words (especially boundary words)
   - Thorough use of notations, symbols, and abbreviations

(2) Time yourself and aim to complete each diagram in approximately 60 to 90 seconds (although your first few diagrams may take considerably longer as you get comfortable). By the time you take your official test, your diagramming time should be approximately 30 to 60 seconds.

After you are done with the entire set, view the sample diagrams that follow. Diagrams will vary, of course. Your diagrams do not need to look exactly like the samples, but carefully consider any large discrepancies.

1. Environmentalist: The national energy commission's current plan calls for the construction of six new nuclear power plants during the next decade. The commission argues that these plants are extremely safe and will have minimal environmental impact on their surrounding communities. However, all six nuclear power plants will be located far from densely populated areas. Clearly, the government is tacitly admitting that these plants do pose a serious health risk to humans.

    Which of the following, if true, most seriously weakens the environmentalist's claim of an unspoken government admission?

2. "Conflict diamonds" are diamonds for which the revenue derived from their sale is used to fund wars or other violent activities. All of the diamonds extracted from the Kugura mine are certified as "conflict free" by a specially appointed government panel. Therefore, consumers can be certain that the money they spend on Kugura diamonds will not be used to fund violent conflict.

    Which of the following, if true, most significantly strengthens the conclusion above?

3. Recently, the tuition at most elite private colleges has been rising faster than inflation. Even before these increases, many low and middle income families were unable to afford the full tuition costs for their children at these institutions of higher learning. With the new tuition increases, these colleges will soon cater solely to students with affluent family backgrounds.

    Which of the following, if true, most seriously weakens the argument that the colleges in question will give strongly preferential treatment to wealthy students?

4. Studies show that impoverished families give away a larger percentage of their income in charitable donations than wealthy families do. As a result, fundraising consultants recommend that charities direct their marketing efforts toward individuals and families from lower socioeconomic classes in order to maximize the dollar value of incoming donations.

    Which of the following best explains why the consultants' reasoning is flawed?

5. Estimated mileage for a new vehicle assumes that the operator will never exceed sixty miles per hour, encounter traffic, or operate the air conditioner. Because these things do happen in practice, the actual mileage of the vehicle is often significantly lower than the estimates noted on the vehicle's window sticker. To rectify this discrepancy, the Environmental Protection Agency has mandated that by 2008, window stickers must reflect actual, rather than theoretical, mileage, a change that is expected to result in an average decline of twelve percent for city driving and eight percent for highway driving.

    Which of the following must be true on the basis of the statements above?

6. A study on higher education states that when parents pay 100 percent of their child's education costs, the child has a twenty-five percent chance of graduating from college. However, if the students themselves pay the entire cost of their education, they have a seventy-five percent graduation rate. Thus, in order to improve graduation rates, parents should refuse to financially contribute to the college educations of their children.

    The conclusion drawn above is based on the assumption that _____.

7. Two-dimensional bar codes are omni-directional, meaning that, unlike one-dimensional bar codes, they can be scanned from any direction. Additionally, two-dimensional bar codes are smaller and can store more data than their one-dimensional counterparts. Despite such advantages, two-dimensional bar codes account for a much smaller portion of total bar code usage than one-dimensional bar codes.

    Which of the following, if true, would best explain the discrepancy above?

8. Whenever a consumer product is declared illegal but the product remains available, a black market inevitably develops. In the United States during the 1920's, for example, a black market for alcohol developed during the Prohibition period. During this period, many organized crime groups grew tremendously more powerful through their black market activities distributing alcohol.

    If the statements above are true, which of the following most significantly weakens the contention that a black market will develop if a product is declared illegal when it still remains available?

9. College officials have recognized that students who do not declare a major by sophomore year are more likely to leave school without graduating. As a result, many colleges around the country are devoting more time and money to help students choose a major. In fact, some schools are spending more than half a million dollars annually to ensure their students do not remain undecided.

    Which of the following, if true, taken together with the information above, best supports the assertion that colleges are saving money by encouraging their underclassmen to choose a major?

10. Editorial: The rash of recent shootings has highlighted the lack of security in our schools. However, arming teachers is a poor solution to this serious problem. Because distraught students will be aware that their teachers possess weapons, permitting guns in the classroom will increase the chances that a conflict that could have been resolved through dialogue will escalate to violence.

    Which of the following, if true, would most strengthen the editorial's conclusion?

1:

Plnt = ↑ hlth rsk to ppl

All plnts far frm pop areas	Comm.: plnts safe, ↓ enviro impct

NEC: 6 nw plnt over nxt 10 yr

2:

$ frm K diam → no war/violence

K diam cert. by gov: NOT confl. diam	
Confl diam = $ usd for war	

3:

Soon, priv. coll only have $$$ students

Tuition ↑ > inflation Even before ↑, low & mid $ fams can't afford	

4:

Cons: to ↑ donations, mkt to ↓ $ ppl

↓ $ ppl donate ↑ % of inc than ↑ $ ppl	

5:

? (no conclusion given)

Est. mile: no traffic, no AC, ↓ 60 mph BUT actual mile. ↓ EPA: by 08, must give actual → avg 12% ↓ city & avg. 8% ↓ hghwy	

Note that this problem has no conclusion given. You may use a question mark or simply leave the top line blank; you do not need to write out "no conclusion given."

6:

To ↑ grad rate, parents shd NOT pay for kids

Study: if parent pays 100%, 25%
   of kids grad
   If kid pays 100%, 75% grad

7:

?

2D bar codes = scan any
dir. (unlike 1D BC)

2D smaller, store ↑ data

BUT 2D ↓↓ % of mkt
than 1D

8:

If st* = illegal but still avail, blck mrkt
will develop

Prohibition (US, '20s, blck
mrkt for alcohol)

Crime ↑ power due to Pro.

[What if it's st ppl don't really want?]

*Note: "st" is an abbreviation for "something."
Also, you do not need to describe Prohibition in your notes if you are already familiar with it.

9:

Coll save $ by encour stud pick major

stud w/o* major ↓ grad

coll spend $, time to help

some coll > $0.5 M/yr

*Note: "w/o" is an abbreviation for "without."

10:

don't arm teachers	
b/c* stud know teach have guns, ↑ chance of conflict → violence	↑ schl shoot

*Note: "b/c" is an abbreviation for "because."

You may need to employ the "Therefore" test to identify the conclusion on this problem. Is the chain of logic represented by (A) or (B) below?

(A) There is a higher chance that conflict will escalate to violence; therefore, we should not arm teachers

(B) We should not arm teachers; therefore there is a higher chance that conflict will escalate to violence

From the language in the argument, the author believes that (A) reflects the proper chain of events. Thus, the final claim in sequence (A) is the conclusion (*we should not arm teachers*).

Chapter 3
of
CRITICAL REASONING

GENERAL STRATEGY

In This Chapter . . .

- Overview of Question Types
- Identifying the Question Type
- "EXCEPT" Questions
- "Fill in the Blank" Questions
- Boundary Words in the Argument
- Extreme Words in the Argument
- General Answer Choice Strategy: Process of Elimination
- Boundary and Extreme Words in the Answer Choices

QUESTION TYPES

The next piece of each Critical Reasoning puzzle is the QUESTION that follows the argument. You can expect several types of questions on the GMAT. The four major question types are as follows:

(1) Find the Assumption
(2) Draw a Conclusion
(3) Strengthen the Conclusion
(4) Weaken the Conclusion

Notice that three of the four major question types involve finding the conclusion in order to answer the question, and the fourth requires us to find the conclusion itself among the answer choices. Clearly, the conclusion is the most important part of each argument!

You may also encounter any of seven minor question types, in the following rough order of frequency:

• Explain an Event or Discrepancy
• Analyze the Argument Structure
• Evaluate the Conclusion
• Resolve a Problem
• Provide an Example
• Restate the Conclusion
• Mimic the Argument

Identifying the Question Type

In addition to giving you clues about the conclusion, the question stem will give you some indication as to the nature of the question.

When reading any question stem, you should try to classify the problem. You will become familiar with each question type in later chapters. When the question stem makes the question type evident, you should be able to adopt the appropriate approach right away.

For example, consider the following question stem:

Which of the following is an assumption on which the argument depends?

This question stem identifies the question as a **Find the Assumption** question. Thus, as we diagram, we should proactively think about assumptions, or unstated gaps necessary to connect the premises to the conclusion.

Here is another common question stem:

Which of the following conclusions can most properly be drawn from the information above?

This question stem identifies the question as a **Draw a Conclusion** question. As we diagram, we know that we will not be given a conclusion. Some or all of the premises must support a conclusion that will be provided in one of the answer choices.

The vast majority of question stems will provide some value, and for this reason the question stem should be read first. However, some question stems may not be as helpful in determining the correct approach to the problem. If the question stem is not immediately helpful or the question type is difficult to identify, do not dwell on the issue. Simply go ahead and diagram the argument; afterwards, you can re-examine the question. In these cases, the process of diagramming will generally clarify the question stem.

"EXCEPT" Questions

Sometimes the GMAT will make a question more complex by using the word EXCEPT. This is <u>not</u> a new question type. The GMAT can manipulate all existing question types by using the EXCEPT formulation. In order to clarify the question stem, rephrase the EXCEPT statement into a question, inserting the word "NOT" and eliminating the word "EXCEPT".

Rephrase EXCEPT questions to make them easier to understand.

Each of the following helps to explain event X EXCEPT:
should be rephrased as: Four answer choices help to explain event X and one does NOT. <u>Which one does NOT explain event X?</u>

Each of the following weakens the conclusion EXCEPT:
should be rephrased as: Four answer choices weaken the conclusion and one does NOT. <u>Which one does NOT weaken the conclusion?</u>

Each of the following strengthens the conclusion EXCEPT:
should be rephrased as: Four answer choices strengthen the conclusion and one does NOT. <u>Which one does NOT strengthen the conclusion?</u>

Each of the following makes the argument logically correct EXCEPT:
should be rephrased as: Four answer choices make the argument logically correct and one does NOT. <u>Which one does NOT make the argument logically correct?</u>

Note that EXCEPT questions do not mean "find the opposite." For example, if we know that a statement *does not strengthen* the conclusion, we do not know whether it *weakens* the conclusion. The statement might indeed weaken the conclusion. Alternatively, the statement could be neutral or beyond the scope of the argument, neither strengthening nor weakening the conclusion.

"Fill in the Blank" Questions

The GMAT may also make a question a bit more complex by structuring it as a "Fill in the Blank" question. Once again, this is not a new type of question. "Fill in the Blank" is simply a disguised version of a question type listed at the beginning of this chapter. These questions are sometimes harder to categorize than the more typical examples. Once you recognize that a "Fill in the Blank" question is of a certain type, you can use the standard strategies associated with that type.

Boundary Words in the Argument

For any question, it is helpful to focus your attention on the BOUNDARY words and phrases provided in the argument. These words and phrases narrow the scope of a premise. For example:

Premise: The percentage of literate adults has increased.

The boundary word *percentage* limits the scope of the premise. It restricts the meaning to percentage only, as opposed to the actual number of literate adults. (We do not know whether the actual number has increased.) The boundary word *adults* also limits the scope of the premise. It restricts the meaning to adults only, as opposed to the total population or children. Finally, the word *literate* obviously restricts the category of adults that has proportionally increased.

Here is another example:

Conclusion: Controversial speech should be allowed, provided it does not incite major violence.

The boundary phrase *provided it does not incite major violence* limits the scope of the conclusion. It restricts the meaning to <u>some</u> types of controversial speech, as opposed to <u>all</u> types of controversial speech. The boundary word *major* limits the exception—controversial speech should not be allowed when it incites <u>major</u> violence, as opposed to <u>any</u> violence.

Boundary words and phrases are vital because they provide nuances to the argument. These nuances will often be manipulated in the answer choices of Critical Reasoning questions. In other words, these nuances can single-handedly make some answer choices correct or incorrect. Therefore, in your diagram, be sure to include boundary words and underline them or capitalize them for emphasis. This will help you identify answer choices that try to trick you on the argument boundaries.

For example, in an argument that contains the premise *the percentage of literate adults has increased*, an incorrect answer choice may include a reference to the <u>number</u> of literate adults, as opposed to the <u>percentage</u>. For this question, make note of this and any other answer choice that attempts to trick you on the difference between *number* and *percentage*. More generally, be aware of any such boundary or limiting word that the GMAT may use to try to trick you.

Boundary words limit the scope of an argument and can be useful in identifying incorrect answer choices.

*Manhattan*GMAT*Prep
the new standard

Extreme Words in the Argument

Another general strategy for all Critical Reasoning questions involves EXTREME words and phrases in the body of the argument. Extreme words, such as *always, never, all,* and *none,* are the opposite of boundary words—they make the argument very broad or far-reaching.

Using extreme words opens up an argument unreasonably, making it very susceptible to attack. For example:

> Conclusion: Sugar is never healthy for anyone trying to lose weight.

The extreme word *never* unreasonably opens up this argument, placing no limitation on the claim that sugar is unhealthy. A more moderate conclusion would argue that sugar is *usually unhealthy*, or that *excessive sugar is unhealthy*. The extreme word *anyone* further opens up this argument. A more moderate conclusion might be that this claim applies to *most* people trying to lose weight.

You should note any extreme language used in premises or conclusions. Since good GMAT arguments rarely contain extreme words, any such words that you find will likely be very useful in responding to the question. You may even want to highlight these extreme terms somehow—for example, by putting an exclamation mark (!) next to them.

Note: this strategy applies to extreme words *only in the argument*. Correct answers <u>can</u> contain extreme words, though you will need to find direct support for the extreme language in the argument.

General Answer Choice Strategy: Process of Elimination

For many Critical Reasoning questions, the correct answer may not be completely clear upon first inspection. However, after you apply criteria that we will discuss in later chapters, it will become clear to you that certain answer choices are incorrect.

For any Critical Reasoning question, it is important to practice the process of elimination using your scratch paper. DO NOT simply eliminate answer choices in your head! As you go through many different questions during the test, it is very difficult to keep straight which answer choices you have ruled out. You do not want to find yourself re-evaluating answers that you have already eliminated!

By the end of the verbal section of the GMAT, your scratch paper should be filled with columns or rows of "A–E" with incorrect answer choices crossed out and correct answers circled. You should practice using your scratch paper in this way so that you are completely comfortable using the scratch booklet provided to you when taking the GMAT.

Even if you believe you have found the correct answer, always check all of the answer choices. You may find that another answer choice is potentially correct, and you will have to rethink your initial choice.

Boundary and Extreme Words in the Answer Choices

Boundary and extreme words also appear in the answer choices. They are just as important as boundary and extreme words in the body of the argument, though for a different reason. Extreme words in the answer choices *usually* make those answer choices incorrect (unless, of course, the argument justifies the use of extreme words).

A correct answer choice must be 100% true. As long as we interpret the words legitimately, such a choice must be valid no matter which way we interpret it. This principle gives us an approach to evaluating answer choices. When you see boundary or extreme words in an answer choice, ask yourself, "What is the most **extreme example** I can think of that would still fit the wording of this answer choice?" Then, using the conclusion and the question asked, see whether your extreme example allows you to eliminate that answer choice.

For example, an answer choice might say:

> (A) Bees live longer than mayflies do.

What are some ways of interpreting this information? Perhaps mayflies live for one second and bees live for one hundred years. This possibility is valid, because the statement *bees live longer than mayflies* is still true. We could also say that mayflies live for one second and bees live for two seconds. Depending on the conclusion and the question, it may be useful to have either an extremely large difference in the life spans or a ridiculously small difference.

Here is another possible answer choice:

> (D) Some teachers leave the profession entirely within three years of beginning their teaching careers.

You might choose to address one of two different boundaries here. The word *some* refers to some number of teachers but does not specify the size of the group. The phrase *within three years* refers to a period of time but does not specify the exact length of time.

If you choose to address the word *some*, you could say that 1% of teachers leave within three years, or that 99% of teachers do so. Either way, the statistics still fit the criterion that *some* teachers do this. Suppose the conclusion asserted that new teacher turnover is having a major impact on the industry. If only 1% of new teachers leave within three years, then new teacher turnover will probably not have much of an impact.

Alternatively, you could interpret *within three years* to mean that many teachers in this category leave after 1 day of teaching. You could also imagine that many teachers in this category leave after 2 years and 364 days of teaching. Again, either way, the statistics still fit the criterion that new teachers leave the profession *within 3 years* of beginning their careers. Depending upon the conclusion and the question, you would then try to disprove answer choices by using these extreme interpretations.

Extreme words, such as *only* or *never*, can appear in correct answers. However, those same extreme words, or their equivalents, must be in the original argument. If the answer choice uses an extreme word that is not explicitly supported by the text of the argument, you should eliminate that choice.

Think about **extreme examples** when you evaluate answer choices with boundary or extreme words.

Chapter 4
of

CRITICAL REASONING

FIND THE
ASSUMPTION

In This Chapter . . .

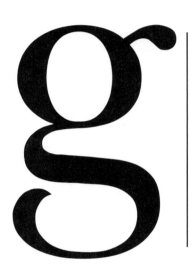

- Find the Assumption Overview
- Close Ties to the Conclusion
- Categories of Assumptions
- Wrong Answer Choice Types
- LEN: The Least Extreme Negation Technique (Advanced)

FIND THE ASSUMPTION

Find the Assumption questions ask you to identify an assumption upon which the argument is based. The question stem most commonly uses the words *assumption* or *assume*, though it may also use other words such as *flaw* or *questionable*, and it may take a number of forms:

> Which of the following is an assumption on which the commissioner's plan depends?

> The argument above relies on which of the following assumptions?

The question stem may also be slightly more subtle:

> The conclusion above would be properly drawn if it were true that _____.

Recall the basic structure of GMAT arguments:

Premises + (Assumptions) = Conclusion

Remember that the argument does not claim merely that the given conclusion is valid, but that the specific premises in the argument <u>lead to</u> the given conclusion. Thus, assumptions serve as a <u>necessary</u> bridge between the premises and the conclusion. The assumption is <u>required</u> in order for the conclusion to be valid.

Close Ties to the Conclusion

As you try to identify the appropriate assumption, you should look for the assumption to:

> (1) bridge a gap between any premise and the conclusion, and
> (2) support/strengthen/validate the conclusion.

The correct answer must be necessary in order for the conclusion to be valid, but the answer does not have to be the <u>only</u> necessary assumption. In other words, the right answer is often "necessary but not sufficient." For example:

> My cat won top prize at the cat show last year. Therefore, she will win again this year.

The author makes many assumptions in this argument: The author's cat will be entered in this year's show. The author's cat will be eligible to win the top prize. The author's cat will still be better than all of the other cats from last year's show, and it will beat out any new cats who may be entered this year. And so on.

Any one of the above assumptions could serve as the correct answer, because each one is <u>necessary</u> in order for the author to believe his or her conclusion. In other words, if the assumption in the correct answer were <u>not</u> true, you could <u>reject</u> the conclusion on that basis alone. For example, if we learned that no cat is allowed to win the top prize two years in a row, then clearly the author's cat is not going to win this year's prize.

The correct answer choice in an assumption question must be necessary to the conclusion of the argument.

At the same time, NONE of the assumptions listed is <u>sufficient by itself</u> to prove that the author's cat will definitely win the prize this year. For instance, if the author's cat *is* eligible to win the prize this year, that does not mean it will definitely do so. The correct answer does not need to make the conclusion definitely true. Indeed, most of the time, the correct answer will only make the conclusion somewhat more likely to be true.

Consider the following example:

> When news periodicals begin forecasting a recession, people tend to spend less money on discretionary purchases. Therefore, the perceived threat of recession decreases the willingness of people to purchase products that they regard as optional or luxury goods.

> The argument above assumes that _____.

> (A) there are more luxury goods available after a recession is forecast
> (B) recently, the threat of recession has been increasingly publicized as news periodicals have grown more pervasive
> (C) most people do not regularly read news periodicals
> (D) people's perception of the threat of recession increases when news periodicals begin forecasting a recession
> (E) the people who spent the most money before a recession was forecast were among those who curtailed their spending after the recession became apparent

To answer this question, first diagram the argument and identify the conclusion.

> prcvd thrt of rec. → ↓ ppl spndg $ on lux. stuff
> _____
> nws prdcl forcst rec. →
> ppl spend ↓ on discret.
> stuff

The correct assumption must bridge a gap between a premise and the conclusion: how do you make the logical leap from news periodicals forecasting a recession to the perceived threat of recession? The only answer choice here that bridges this gap and thus validates the conclusion is **(D)**:

(D) people's perception of the threat of recession increases when news periodicals begin forecasting a recession

Note that the premise states that the decreased spending is due to the fact that news periodicals are forecasting a recession. Furthermore, the expressions *perceived threat of recession* (in the passage) and *perception of the threat of recession* (in the answer choice) are essentially synonymous. Finally, the answer choice logically fills a gap between a premise and the conclusion:

*Manhattan*GMAT*Prep
the new standard

Premise:	News periodicals publish the forecast of a recession
Assumption:	*As a result, people's perception of the threat of a recession increases*
Premise:	People spend less money on discretionary items
Conclusion:	Therefore, the perceived threat causes people to spend less money

You might be surprised at how little the assumption assumes. It merely makes explicit a logical step in the argument: when news periodicals begin forecasting a recession, people's perception of a threat of recession increases. Also, note what happens if we negate the assumption and say that perception of the threat does NOT increase when the periodicals forecast a recession:

Premise:	News periodicals publish the recession forecast
Negated	
Assumption:	*However, people's perception of the threat does NOT increase*
Premise:	As a result of the forecast, people spend less money on discretionary items
Conclusion:	Therefore, the perceived threat causes people to spend less money

In this case, the conclusion becomes nonsensical. If the publication of the forecast leads to less spending but does *not* lead to an increased perception of the threat, then how can we reasonably conclude that the perceived threat is what causes people to spend less money?

As you can see, negating an assumption is a powerful technique. If an answer choice in a Find An Assumption question is negated and the argument becomes nonsensical, then the answer choice is almost certainly <u>correct</u>. This idea should make sense; after all, an assumption is <u>necessary</u> for the argument to hold.

Just as we have demonstrated why (**D**) must be the answer, we can also analyze the errors in each incorrect answer choice.

Answer choice (**A**) describes a possible result after a recession is forecast, but that possible result has nothing to do with whether people will reduce discretionary spending because of the news periodicals' reporting of the threat of a recession.

Answer choice (**B**) describes a trend that may be true, but the claim that forecasts published in news periodicals cause people to reduce spending does not require the rate of publication to be on the rise.

Answer choice (**C**) is a statement that would <u>weaken</u> the conclusion. If people are not reading the periodicals, then it does not make sense to claim that people are changing their spending habits as a result of what the periodicals publish.

Answer choice (**E**) describes a possible result after a recession actually occurs. The conclusion is concerned with the <u>perceived</u> threat of a recession, not what might happen due to an actual recession.

All of these answer choices can be properly eliminated because of their incorrect relationship to the conclusion.

Before reading the answer choices, think about assumptions upon which an argument's conclusion is based.

FIND THE ASSUMPTION

You might have projected a different assumption as the answer to this question. For example, another assumption essential to this argument is that the underlying economic forces causing the periodicals to forecast a recession do not <u>themselves</u> cause discretionary spending to drop. In other words, there must not be an outside factor leading both to the forecasts and the spending decrease. An argument might depend on several assumptions, any one of which could serve as the correct answer. However, <u>only one</u> of these correct assumptions will be given to you in the answer choices. It does not hurt to brainstorm possible assumptions (in fact, it is often useful to do this!), but remember that the correct answer may be an assumption you did not think of ahead of time. Always keep an open mind as you eliminate answer choices.

Categories of Assumptions

The correct answer to Find the Assumption questions almost always falls into one of the following four categories.

<u>1. Assumptions can serve to fill in a logic gap.</u>

Most assumptions simply fill in gaps in the logic or sequence of an argument. They provide additional premises that are needed to draw the conclusion, given the premises in the argument. These assumptions answer the question, "How do we logically get from Point A to Point B?"

The premises in "logic gap" arguments will tend to be fact-based or provide background information. Only occasionally will the premises reflect an opinion or claim of some sort. The arguments will also tend to tie one particular premise to the conclusion with language such as *therefore, for this reason, because*, etc. The right answer will generally address the gap between a particular premise and the conclusion.

> Andrew weighs less than 200 pounds. Therefore, he cannot have a successful career as a racecar driver.

In order to make the logical leap from Point A to Point B—that Andrew is under 200 pounds and therefore cannot have a successful career as a racecar driver—we must insert an additional premise. This unstated premise is an assumption.

The correct answer choice might be as follows:

> In order to have a successful career as a racecar driver, one must weigh at least 200 pounds.

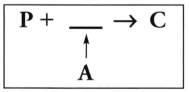

In this case, P represents **weighs less than 200 pounds** and C represents **cannot be a successful racecar driver**. An assumption—call it A—sits between P and C. This A is the assumption that Andrew cannot be a successful racecar driver <u>unless</u> he weighs 200 pounds or more. Note that if that assumption is not true, then the whole argument falls apart.

Logic gap assumptions help connect Point A (a premise) with Point B (a conclusion).

2. Assumptions can establish the feasibility of the premises of the argument.

Assumptions of this type indicate that the premises can actually occur in the way the argument describes—regardless of how uncertain or tenuous these premises are in the original argument. For instance, if a premise claims that *applying this pesticide will kill termites*, then we are assuming that this pesticide CAN kill termites. "Feasibility" means "ability to occur or to be true."

Generally, the premises in "feasibility" arguments reflect opinions or claims of some sort. The right answer will address the assumption that these opinions are true or that a sequence of events can occur in the way the argument assumes it will.

> Sidney's get-rich-quick scheme is sure to succeed. He will buy undervalued properties in foreclosure. Then he will resell the properties to a local real estate developer and generate large profits.

This argument *assumes* that undervalued properties in foreclosure actually exist and that Sidney can find them. It also assumes that local real estate developers will want to buy such properties from Sidney and will be willing to pay more than he paid in the first place. Sidney is assuming these claims and that the sequence of events will take place as described.

One correct answer choice might be: Undervalued properties exist in foreclosure and easily can be found and purchased by Sidney.

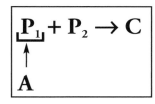

In this case, P_1 represents *he will buy undervalued properties in foreclosure*. P_2 represents *he will sell these properties to a developer for large profits*, and C represents *Sidney's get-rich-quick scheme is sure to succeed*. Statement A makes explicit the assumption that Sidney actually CAN buy undervalued properties in foreclosure.

Note that this particular correct answer does not establish all of the missing assumptions outlined above. It is enough for the correct answer to address one assumption. Indeed, the answer could just as easily have been an assumption that bolstered claim P_2 rather than P_1. The key to any assumption is that if the negation is *not* true—that is, if these properties do not exist or cannot be easily found and purchased by Sidney—then the conclusion falls apart.

3. Assumptions can eliminate alternate paths to reach a given conclusion.

Many GMAT arguments contain linear logic paths: P_1 and P_2 are true, therefore C is true. However, the speaker often ignores the possibility of a *different path to reach the same conclusion.*

Feasibility assumptions generally revolve around bolstering a flimsy but necessary claim in the premises.

FIND THE ASSUMPTION

These arguments will often use some type of <u>superlative</u> qualifier in the conclusion. That is, we are told that the given path is the *only* way to reach a goal, or the *best* or *worst* way. In order for such a claim to be true, there cannot be *another* way, or a *better* or *worse* way.

> A magazine published an article proclaiming that one can get a promotion by playing golf with one's boss. Kevin concludes that the best way for him to get promoted is to take golf lessons and join his boss's country club.

Notice that the conclusion uses the phrase *best way*. This ignores the many other (probably more reliable) ways that Kevin could get himself noticed and promoted. In other words, the argument assumes that there is <u>no better way</u> for him to get promoted than to play golf with his boss.

The correct answer choice might be: There are no other better ways to gain a promotion than to play golf with one's boss.

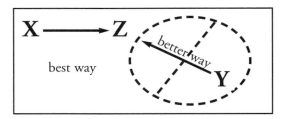

In this case, X represents *playing golf with one's boss* and Z represents *getting a promotion*. The arrow indicates that X is the best way to get to Z. Y makes explicit that there is no <u>better way</u> for Kevin to accomplish his goal.

Note that, once again, other assumptions are made in this argument. For example, Kevin also assumes that his boss plays golf, but this necessary assumption would not also appear in the answer choices. Only one correct assumption will be given in the answer choices.

<u>4. Assumptions can eliminate alternate causes for a given conclusion.</u>

Many GMAT conclusions are statements of cause and effect. For some of these cause-and-effect conclusions, the given premises simply note a correlation between two phenomena, without commenting on any causal relationships between them.

A correlation means that two things occur together, without necessarily indicating why. For example, a premise might say this:

> Scientists have discovered that people with Elmer's disease have elevated levels of elastomer in their blood.

What do we know? Elmer's disease and elastomer show up together. In other words, these two phenomena are correlated. But we do not know whether elevated levels of elastomer causes Elmer's disease, or whether Elmer's disease causes elevated levels of elastomer. There is even a third possibility: both Elmer's disease and elevated levels of elastomer could be caused by some third, unknown factor (perhaps a genetic defect). In short, correlation is not the same as causation.

A conclusion that states that one particular path is the best way to achieve an end assumes that other means of achieving the same end are not as good.

The conclusion of the argument could be this:

> The scientists concluded that a person without Elmer's disease but with elevated levels of elastomer in the blood is likely to develop Elmer's disease in the future.

In this case, X represents *elevated levels of elastomer* and Z represents *Elmer's disease*. The arrow indicates that X causes Z.

What are the scientists assuming? They are assuming that the correlation they observe results from X: the elevated levels of elastomer.

However, what if Elmer's disease is the cause? What if Z causes X? We would see the same correlation between the two phenomena (the disease and the chemical in the blood). In concluding that elevated elastomer levels cause Elmer's disease, the scientists are actually assuming that Elmer's disease is NOT the cause of the elastomer levels. In other words, the assumption is that the causality does NOT run the other way, from Z to X:

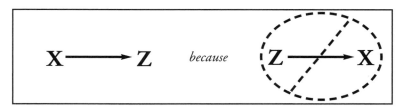

(In addition, the scientists are assuming that a third factor is not the cause of both Z and X, but the correct answer usually hinges only on negating the reverse causality.)

Consider another example.

> Economists have noticed that countries with more developed cultures of entrepreneurship and risk-taking have higher economic growth rates. Therefore, they have concluded that cultures of entrepreneurship and risk-taking generate higher rates of growth over time.

The premise states that *more developed cultures of entrepreneurship and risk-taking* occur alongside *higher economic growth rates*. The conclusion asserts that such cultures <u>cause</u> higher growth rates.

The conclusion simply assumes a certain causation and ignores the possibility that the reverse might be true. Perhaps higher economic growth rates create more opportunities for entrepreneurship and risk-taking, increasing the development of these qualities over time. In order for the conclusion to be valid, the researchers are *assuming* that the reverse model of causation is, in fact, false.

The correct answer choice might be this: Higher growth rates in an economy do not contribute to a more highly developed culture of entrepreneurship and risk-taking.

In short, if a premise provides a correlation between X and Z, and the conclusion provides a causality in one direction (X causes Z), then the assumption you are usually looking for is that Z does NOT cause X. That is, you must rule out the causality in the other direction.

Wrong Answer Choice Types

In GMAT critical reasoning questions, you will find several common categories of wrong answer choices. You should learn to recognize these categories. Of course, you do not need to classify every wrong answer you see during the test itself. Instead, you will use your familiarity with wrong answer types to eliminate very tempting (but wrong!) answer choices.

On a Find the Assumption question, you have to find a choice that <u>must be true</u> in order for the author to reach the conclusion from the given premises.

Take a look again at a previous sample argument:

> Economists have noticed that countries with more developed cultures of entrepreneurship and risk-taking have higher economic growth rates. Therefore, they have concluded that cultures of entrepreneurship and risk-taking generate higher rates of growth over time.

We have already discussed what the right answer might look like. The typical wrong answer is often "out of scope" or "irrelevant"—but what do those terms actually mean?

A. No Tie to the Conclusion

The most common type of wrong answer choice provides "No Tie to the Conclusion." That is, the answer choice provides an "assumption" that is *not actually necessary* for the conclusion to be logically valid. Thus, the answer choice is not a true assumption, although it often discusses something related to a premise.

In relation to the sample argument above, a "No Tie to the Conclusion" answer choice might say this:

> Countries with high economic growth rates typically have low unemployment rates.

This choice starts from a concept in the argument (*economic growth rates*) but then discusses something unrelated to the conclusion (*unemployment rates*). Wrong answers of this type are sometimes obviously wrong. At other times, however, they can be very tempting, because they repeat information from the argument and explore a tangential line of thinking that many test-takers might incorrectly consider.

A common sub-type in the No Tie to the Conclusion category is **Breaks up a Category**. Suppose you are given this argument:

> Because fewer people are visiting the local state park, the park is not earning enough money from entrance fees. A survey indicated that young adults are more likely to visit the local state park than are middle-aged or elderly adults. Thus, the state should advertise the park in publications aimed at young adults.

Certain wrong answer choice patterns occur frequently—be on the lookout for them!

If you are asked a Find the Assumption question, a "Breaks up a Category" wrong answer choice might say this:

> Middle-aged adults are more likely to visit the state park in question than are elderly adults.

This cannot be the correct answer to a Find The Assumption question. While the argument does mention both middle-aged and elderly adults, the conclusion in question does not address this distinction. Rather, the argument draws a distinction between (1) young adults and (2) middle-aged or elderly adults. Note that *middle-aged or elderly adults* serves as <u>one</u> logical category in the original argument. Therefore, any distinctions made between middle-aged and elderly adults are not relevant to the argument. The answer choice above does not provide a necessary foundation for the conclusion.

Whenever you encounter an answer choice that Breaks up a Category or otherwise has No Tie to the Conclusion, eliminate that choice.

B. Wrong Direction

Another common type of incorrect answer choice goes in the "Wrong Direction." That is, the answer choice provides the opposite of what you are looking for. Consider this argument again:

> Economists have noticed that countries with more developed cultures of entrepreneurship and risk-taking have higher economic growth rates. Therefore, they have concluded that cultures of entrepreneurship and risk-taking generate higher rates of growth over time.

A "Wrong Direction" answer choice in a Find the Assumption question might say this:

> Higher economic growth rates in a given country tend to result in increased levels of entrepreneurship and risk-taking.

"Wrong Direction" choices can be very tempting if you are not reading carefully, because they often contain all the right keywords. They can also be very tempting on convoluted or confusing arguments, as in the example above.

If you consider this answer choice, you will find that this choice actually weakens the argument! The argument states that X (risk-taking culture) causes Z (higher growth rates) because X and Z are correlated. The assumption we are looking for should *rule out* the possibility that Z causes X, but this wrong answer actually *asserts* that Z causes X. This alternative model provides a good rationale for the premise, but it undermines the conclusion.

C. Switching Terms

A third type of incorrect answer choice "Switches Terms." That is, the answer choice replaces a fundamental term in the argument with something that seems like a synonym, if you are not paying attention. The choice may also introduce an extreme word that is not justified in the argument.

A correct assumption will always support the conclusion. If an answer choice on a Find the Assumption question *undermines* the conclusion, the choice is wrong.

A common switch is between hard numbers and proportions or percentages. Suppose you are given the following argument:

> 90% of Company X's employees take some form of public transportation to get to work. Of those who take public transportation, however, fewer than 5% take the bus. Therefore, Company X should not subsidize bus fares for its employees.

A "Switching Terms" choice on a Find the Assumption question might say this:

> Only a small number of people would benefit from Company X's bus fare subsidies.

This answer choice is wrong because it switches terms. We know that only a small PROPORTION of Company X's employees take the bus (in fact, it is less than 90% of 5%, or 4.5%). However, the absolute NUMBER of those employees could be large, if Company X has tens or hundreds of thousands of employees. **Proportions and hard numbers are different**; be sure to keep them straight.

In summary, the three types listed above (No Ties to the Conclusion, Wrong Direction, and Switching Terms) account for many of the wrong answers on Find the Assumption questions. Occasionally, a wrong answer choice will employ different modes of attack, repeating language from the argument in other deceptive ways.

- **Addresses Premise Only**: This type explains or leads to a premise, rather than to the conclusion. The right answer needs to address the conclusion.

- **Follow On**: This type follows from the conclusion instead of identifying an assumption that underlies the conclusion.

Again, do not attempt to classify wrong answers as a first line of attack. These categories may be useful if you need to decide between two tempting answer choices in the final stage of a problem.

LEN: The Least Extreme Negation Technique (Advanced)

What should you do when two (or more) answer choices are very tempting? Earlier in this chapter, we noted that an argument will fail without its assumptions. Thus, **negating any correct assumption will destroy the argument**. The premises will no longer support the conclusion.

As a result, we can try negating answer choices to see whether the argument fails. This approach is the heart of the Least Extreme Negation (LEN) technique. We simply have to negate the choices carefully. As the name of the technique implies, **you should use the least extreme negation that you possibly can**. After all, an extreme version in the <u>opposite</u> direction will not necessarily impact the argument.

Take a look at the simple example below.

> Sam is currently the deputy mayor of Geneva County. Therefore, Sam should be the next mayor of Geneva when the current mayor retires.
>
> Which of the following is an assumption on which the author relies?

Imagine two possible answer choices:

> (B) Sam is the most honest person in the whole county.
>
> (D) The deputy mayor is always the best person to become the next mayor when a current mayor retires.

Let us start with **(B)**. Honesty would be a good characteristic for a mayor, so this choice is tempting. But is it absolutely <u>necessary</u> for Sam to be the most honest person in the county, if we want to draw the given conclusion? Try negating this answer choice.

You may be tempted to say *Sam is the most DISHONEST person in the whole county,* but this is not a <u>least</u> extreme negation. In fact, it is the <u>most</u> extreme. The least extreme negation might be *Sam is NOT NECESSARILY the most honest person in the whole county.* Does this statement destroy the conclusion? No. You can still argue that Sam should be the next mayor, even if you concede that he is not necessarily the most honest person in the county. If the conclusion can still follow from the premises, even when you insert a least extreme negation of the answer choice, then that answer choice is incorrect.

Let us look at **(D)** instead. The least extreme negation might be *The deputy mayor is NOT NECESSARILY the best person to become the next mayor when a current mayor retires.* Does this statement destroy the argument's support for the conclusion? Yes! The only reason the argument gives for concluding that Sam should be the next mayor is that Sam is currently the deputy mayor. If we then learn that the deputy mayor is not necessarily the best person to take over the job, the given premise no longer supports the conclusion. The conclusion might still be valid, but a substantial amount of the supportive infrastructure for the conclusion has now been negated. We would need <u>new</u> premises to feel comfortable that the conclusion is valid.

Consider a more GMAT-like example:

> For several years, Nighttime News attracted fewer viewers than World News, which broadcasts its show at the same time as Nighttime News. Recently, the producers of Nighttime News added personal interest stories and increased coverage of sports and weather. The two programs now have a roughly equal number of viewers. Clearly, the recent programming changes persuaded viewers to switch from World News to Nighttime News.
>
> Which of the following is an assumption on which the author relies?

To test whether an answer choice provides a necessary assumption, ask yourself whether the conclusion of the argument could still be valid even if the answer choice were NOT true.

(A) Viewers are more interested in sports and weather than in personal interest stories.

(B) The programming content of Nighttime News is more closely aligned with the interests of the overall audience than is the content of World News.

(C) Some World News viewers liked the new Nighttime News programming better than they liked the World News programming.

(D) There are other possible causes for an increase in the number of viewers of Nighttime News, including a recent ad campaign that aired on many local affiliates.

(E) The quality of World News will remain constant even if Nighttime News improves.

Again, we should diagram the argument and identify the conclusion.

Use the LEN technique only when you have two or more attractive answer choices.

As you are reading through the argument, if you think of any possible assumptions on which the conclusion depends, note those below your diagram, in brackets. One assumption is *Nighttime News did not gain its new viewers from some other source or for some other reason.* Another assumption is that *World News did not lose viewers.* These assumptions make the comparisons

Program changes → ppl switch fr WN to NN

| Before: NN < viewers than WN |
| Recent: NN chng: ↑ pers, sprt, weath |
| Now NN = WN viewers |
| [Is NN # ↑ for some other reason? Or maybe WN ↓ ?] |

of viewer numbers valid. However, unfortunately, these assumptions are not contained in any of the answer choices. We will need to look for another assumption.

We can eliminate several answer choices relatively quickly.

Answer choice **(A)** is incorrect because we are trying to support the conclusion that the changes made resulted in World News viewers switching to Nighttime News. Sports, weather, and personal interest stories were all part of those changes. Trying to distinguish among these makes a finer distinction than is necessary to this argument.

Answer choice **(D)** is tempting because it addresses a possible separate cause for the increase in viewers at Nighttime News. However, this answer choice weakens the conclusion. Even if Nighttime News did gain some new viewers for a different reason, some World News viewers could still have switched to Nighttime News due to the new programming changes. If there are other possible reasons for an increase in the number of viewers, it is less likely that the recent programming changes are responsible for drawing new viewers. Remember, an assumption actually supports the conclusion.

Answer choice **(E)** discusses the quality of World News—perhaps, if World News also improves, then Nighttime News will still find itself behind. The problem with this choice is that the changes have already been implemented and the viewership has already changed as a result. The conclusion seeks to explain why the viewership has changed. This choice discusses a future possibility, which cannot affect what has already happened.

In contrast, both answer choices (**B**) and (**C**) seem closely tied to the language of the conclusion. Answer choice (**B**) refers to *programming content* and *interests of the overall audience*. Answer choice (**C**) refers to *viewers* and *programming*.

Now that we have only two attractive answer choices remaining, we should bring in the Least Extreme Negation technique.

Answer choice (**B**) says *The content of Nighttime News is more closely aligned to the interests of the overall audience than is the content of World News.* You may be tempted to negate choice (**B**) with *The content of Nighttime News is LESS closely aligned to the interests of the overall audience than is the content of World News,* but this is not the least extreme way to negate the choice.

The least extreme negation would read *The content of Nighttime News is ABOUT AS ALIGNED AS, or LESS ALIGNED THAN, the content of World News to the interests of the overall audience.* (The opposite of *more* is not *less;* it is *less than or equal to.*) You could also say *The content of Nighttime News is NOT NECESSARILY more closely aligned to the interests of the overall audience than is the content of World News*

Does the least extreme negation harm the argument? Now the shortcomings of answer choice (**B**) become apparent. The choice tells us something about how the broadcasts are catering to the interests of the audience, but it does not discuss whether the content changes would specifically drive viewers from World News to Nighttime News. However, the conclusion hinges on this issue of switching. What difference does it make whether the Nighttime News content is better aligned with viewer interests? Perhaps World News has a famous anchorperson who used to be a sports star at the local university, and for this reason, audiences prefer to watch him or her. Therefore, the least extreme negation does not affect the conclusion.

Answer choice (**C**), on the other hand, MUST be true in order for the conclusion to follow from the premises. Answer choice (**C**) states that *Some World News viewers liked the new Nighttime News programming better than they liked the World News programming... .* The least extreme negation might read *NO World News viewers liked the new Nighttime News programming better than they liked the World News programming.*

Under this negation, the conclusion of the argument would no longer be supported by the premises. While the ratings have certainly changed, the argument claims that they changed <u>because World News viewers switched to Nighttime News</u>. The premises that Nighttime News changed its programming and the viewership subsequently equalized no longer support the conclusion that viewers switched <u>because of the changes in programming</u>. Indeed, under this negation, we would need to believe that the ratings changed for some other reason. This demonstrates how answer choice (**C**) is required by the conclusion and is therefore an assumption of the argument. Answer choice (**C**) is correct.

Be careful as you negate assumptions. Always keep straight whether you are working with the original assumption or the negated version.

More LEN Examples

Remember that Least Extreme Negation is a technique for you to use if you are stuck between two answer choices. Some examples of common ways to apply Least Extreme Negation are listed below.

Always, only, all: insert *Not necessarily.* You can also use *Sometimes... not* in place of *Always,* or *Some... not* in place of *All.*

> (B) Tomatoes are <u>always</u> red.
> LEN: **Tomatoes are NOT NECESSARILY always red.**
> *OR*   **Tomatoes are SOMETIMES NOT red.**

Never, none, not one, not once: change to *At least one* or *at least once.*

> (D) <u>Not one</u> player was late for practice.
> LEN: **AT LEAST ONE player was late for practice.**

Some, a few, several: change to *No* or *None.* (Notice that this may sound extreme!)

> (A) <u>Some</u> cats purr when you pet them.
> LEN: **NO cats purr when you pet them.**

Sometimes, on occasion, often: change to *Never.* (Notice that this may sound extreme!)

> (A) Cats <u>sometimes</u> purr when you pet them.
> LEN: **Cats NEVER purr when you pet them.**

At least, at most, more than, less than: change to the mathematically opposite term.

> (C) She has <u>at least three</u> different job offers.
> LEN: **She has LESS THAN THREE different job offers.**

Best, worst, greatest, smallest, highest: insert *Not necessarily.*

> (E) Beth is the <u>best</u> tennis player in the world.
> LEN: **Beth is NOT NECESSARILY the best tennis player in the world.**

If you are not sure how to negate a particular assumption in a least extreme way, a reasonable approach is to try adding the words **NOT NECESSARILY**.

Certain keywords can simplify the application of LEN. For example, *always* can be negated by using *sometimes not.*

the new standard

Problem Set

Use the skills you have just learned to answer the following Find The Assumption questions. Be sure to diagram each argument. In addition, identify which of the four assumption types is represented by the correct answer: (1) Logic Gap, (2) Feasibility of Premises, (3) Alternate Path, or (4) Alternate Model of Causation. Detailed answers and explanations follow this problem set.

1. Soccer Coach

The local university recently hired a new soccer coach. Although she has several years' worth of coaching experience and is a diligent student of the game, she was never a member of a collegiate soccer team. For this reason, the new coach will be unable to build a successful program.

The argument above is based on which of the following assumptions?

(A) The local university should have hired a former collegiate soccer player as its new coach.
(B) Coaching experience is one of the most crucial factors for coaching success.
(C) The previous coach at the university was dismissed due to her lack of success.
(D) To build a successful soccer program as a coach, one must be a former collegiate soccer player.
(E) The university does not plan to provide the new coach with the resources necessary to build a successful program.

2. MTC & Asthma

Methyltetrachloride (MTC) is a chemical found in some pesticides, glues, and sealants. Exposure to MTC can cause people to develop asthma. In order to halve the nation's asthma rate, the government has announced that it will ban all products containing MTC.

The government's plan to halve the nation's asthma rate relies on which of the following assumptions?

(A) Exposure to MTC is responsible for no less than half of the nation's asthma cases.
(B) Products containing MTC are not necessary to the prosperity of the American economy.
(C) Asthma has reached epidemic proportions.
(D) Exercise and proper nutrition are helpful in maintaining respiratory health.
(E) Dust mites and pet dander cause asthma.

3. Be A Good Driver

Traffic Safety Expert: In order to achieve a substantial reduction in the extremely high number of car accidents in our country, we should implement a radical new safe driving plan. Seat belts and air bags would be eliminated from the driver's side of all automobiles to provide the driver with the strongest possible incentive to drive safely. Further, an electroshock system would administer shocks to the driver if he or she exceeds the speed limit or engages in other unsafe driving practices.

In declaring that the radical new safe driving plan will help to reduce accident rates, the author assumes which of the following?

(A) Many car accidents are caused, at least partially, by naturally occurring conditions such as rain and fog.

(B) Accidents in which one or both participants exceed 60 miles per hour account for a majority of all fatal car accidents.

(C) A significant number of accidents are the result of negligence or other unsafe driving practices on the part of the driver.

(D) To alleviate safety concerns, citizens should be allowed to reinstall their drivers' side seat belts and air bags at their own expense.

(E) If not implemented properly, electroshock systems can cause heart attacks and other health problems.

4. Genetics

Two genes, BRCA1 and BRCA2, are linked to hereditary breast cancer. Therefore, in order to decrease the annual number of mammogram tests administered across a population and to more accurately assess a woman's individual risk of breast cancer, all women should be tested for these genes.

Which of the following is an assumption on which the argument depends?

(A) Some of the women who are tested for the two genes will subsequently undergo mammograms on a less frequent basis than they used to.

(B) The majority of breast cancer patients have no family history of the disease.

(C) Researchers may have identified a third breast cancer gene that is linked with hereditary breast cancer.

(D) Women who have these genes have an 80 percent chance of getting breast cancer, while women who don't have these genes have only a 10 percent chance of getting breast cancer.

(E) The presence of BRCA1 and BRCA2 can explain up to 50 percent of hereditary cases.

5. Intercontinental Bank

Editorial: The Intercontinental Bank should reallocate the voting shares of its members in order to more effectively shape global economic policy. For example, China comprises about 15 percent of the world's gross domestic product but has only a 3 percent voting share, whereas Belgium, with less than 1 percent of the global economy, has a 2 percent share.

Which of the following is an assumption upon which the editorial's authors depend in suggesting a way to more effectively shape global economic policy?

(A) The United States has a larger voting share of the Intercontinental Bank than does China or Belgium.

(B) The specific allocation of voting shares factors into the Intercontinental Bank's effectiveness in shaping global economic policy.

(C) Only voting shares that are precisely proportional to each country's contribution to the global economy are appropriate for the Intercontinental Bank.

(D) The Intercontinental Bank is necessary to the maintenance of a prosperous global economy.

(E) As one of the fastest growing economies, China should have a larger voting share in the Intercontinental Bank.

6. Fresh Start

Advertisement: According to a recent research study, daily use of Fresh Start, a new tooth-paste, reduces the risk of developing dental cavities by over 20 percent. In addition, as a result of a new formula, the use of Fresh Start results in whiter, healthier-looking teeth. Clearly, Fresh Start not only gives your teeth a beautiful look but also provides the most reliable protection against dental cavities.

Which of the following is an assumption in the argument above?

(A) No other toothpaste provides more reliable protection against dental cavities.
(B) Fresh Start's formula does a better job of whitening teeth than do competitors' formulas.
(C) People are just as interested in having beautiful teeth as they are in having healthy teeth.
(D) Fresh Start also prevents other dental disorders, such as gingivitis.
(E) Reliable protection against dental cavities, combined with excellent aesthetic properties, is
   likely to make Fresh Start a popular toothpaste on the market.

7. Exchange Student

Student Advisor: One of our exchange students faced multiple arguments with her parents over the course of the past year. Not surprisingly, her grade point average (GPA) over the same period showed a steep decline. This is just one example of a general truth: problematic family relationships can cause significant academic difficulties for our students.

Which of the following is an assumption underlying the general truism claimed by the Student Advisor?

(A) Last year, the exchange student reduced the amount of time spent on academic work,
   resulting in a lower GPA.
(B) The decline in the GPA of the exchange student was not the reason for the student's argu-
   ments with her parents.
(C) School GPA is an accurate measure of a student's intellectual ability.
(D) If proper measures are not taken, the decline in the student's academic performance may
   become irreversible.
(E) Fluctuations in academic performance are typical for many students.

8. Oil and Ethanol

Country B's oil production is not sufficient to meet its domestic demand. In order to sharply reduce its dependence on foreign sources of oil, Country B recently embarked on a program requiring all of its automobiles to run on ethanol in addition to gasoline. Combined with its oil production, Country B produces enough ethanol from agricultural by-products to meet its cur-rent demand for energy.

Which of the following must be assumed in order to conclude that Country B will succeed in its plan to reduce its dependence on foreign oil?

(A) Electric power is not a superior alternative to ethanol in supplementing automobile gasoline consumption.
(B) In Country B, domestic production of ethanol is increasing more quickly than domestic oil
   production.
(C) Ethanol is suitable for the heating of homes and other applications aside from automobiles.

(D) In Country B, gasoline consumption is not increasing at a substantially higher rate than domestic oil and ethanol production.

(E) Ethanol is as efficient as gasoline in terms of mileage per gallon when used as fuel for automobiles.

9. Housing Insanity

An industry analyst asserted in his recent report that the relative scarcity of housing in a particular market leads to larger than normal increases in price. During the late 1990s, according to the analyst's report, occupancy rates—a measure of the percentage of housing occupied at a given time—in crowded urban markets such as New York and San Francisco hovered around 99.5%., During the same period, housing prices increased by as much as 100% per year, compared to more normal past increases in the range of 5% to 15% per year.

Which of the following is an assumption that supports the analyst's assertion?

(A) In the housing market, there generally must be at least five buyers per seller in order to cause larger than normal increases in price.

(B) Increases in demand often reflect an influx of new buyers into the marketplace or an unusual increase in buying power on the part of the customer.

(C) The U.S. housing market showed a larger than average increase in the 1990s across the country, not just in crowded urban areas.

(D) Price increases do not cause people to withhold their houses from the market in the hopes that prices will increase even further in the future.

(E) A significant rise in housing prices in a specific area may cause some potential buyers to relocate to other, less pricey areas.

10. Movie Money

Studio executives carefully examine how a film performs on its opening weekend in order to determine whether—and how—to invest more in that film. Many decisions, such as increasing the number of screens that show the film and expanding the marketing campaign, are best made after reactions can be gathered from audiences who actually purchased tickets. Therefore, to maximize returns on their marketing investments, studios should initially release all their films on a small number of screens and with a limited advertising campaign.

The plan to maximize returns by initially releasing films on only a small number of screens and limiting advertising depends upon which of the following assumptions?

(A) Large marketing investments made before the opening weekend never eventually yield greater profits than small initial marketing investments.

(B) New advertising techniques, such as Web-based viral marketing, have not substantially reduced the average marketing costs for films.

(C) A film's prior performance in noncommercial settings, such as festivals, is not well correlated with how the general public tends to react to that film.

(D) Across the movie industry, marketing investments do not influence the eventual financial returns of films in predictable ways.

(E) How a film performs during its opening weekend is a strong indicator of the film's financial performance over its lifetime.

1. Soccer Coach

The local university recently hired a new soccer coach. Although she has several years' worth of coaching experience and is a diligent student of the game, she was never a member of a collegiate soccer team. For this reason, the new coach will be unable to build a successful program.

The argument above is based on which of the following assumptions?

(A) Studying the game is not as important as having extensive coaching experience.
(B) Coaching experience is one of the most crucial factors for coaching success.
(C) The previous coach at the university was dismissed due to her lack of success.
(D) To build a successful soccer program as a coach, one must be a former collegiate soccer player.
(E) The university does not plan to provide the new coach with the resources necessary to build a successful program.

The correct answer choice fills in a **LOGIC GAP**.

This argument concludes that, even though the new coach has significant coaching experience and has studied the game, she will not be able to build a successful soccer program because she was never a member of a collegiate soccer team. The argument thus assumes that having been a member of a collegiate soccer team is a prerequisite for success as a soccer coach.

(A) This answer choice provides a finer distinction between two premises: coaching experience and the coach's study of the game. The conclusion does not hinge on these two "positive" premises; rather, the conclusion that the new coach will be unsuccessful is based upon the "negative" premise that she was never on a college soccer team.

(B) The argument discounts the importance of coaching experience for coaching success. If this statement were true, one would conclude that this coach will be more likely to build a successful program.

(C) This choice is outside the scope of the argument. The previous coach's performance has no bearing on the current coach's expected performance.

(D) **CORRECT.** The argument assumes that former experience on a collegiate soccer team is a prerequisite for building a successful program as a coach.

(E) Though it may be true that the university does not plan to provide full resources to the new coach, and while this would certainly make it more difficult for any coach to build a successful program, the choice is outside the scope of this argument. The conclusion states that the coach will not be successful *because* she was never a member of a collegiate soccer team. The conclusion does not address what role the university itself might play in the coach's success (or failure).

2. MTC & Asthma

Methyltetrachloride (MTC) is a chemical found in some pesticides, glues, and sealants. Exposure to MTC can cause people to develop asthma. In order to halve the nation's asthma rate, the government plans to ban all products containing MTC.

The government's plan to halve the nation's asthma rate relies on which of the following assumptions?

(A) Exposure to MTC is responsible for no less than half of the nation's asthma cases.
(B) Products containing MTC are not necessary to the prosperity of the American economy.
(C) Asthma has reached epidemic proportions.
(D) Exercise and proper nutrition are helpful in maintaining respiratory health.
(E) Dust mites and pet dander can also asthma.

The correct answer choice fills in a **LOGIC GAP**.

The government plans to halve the nation's asthma rate by banning products containing MTC. For this plan to succeed, it must be true that MTC causes at least half of the nation's asthma cases.

(A) CORRECT. The government's proposed ban on MTC cannot halve the nation's asthma rate unless MTC is actually the thing responsible for at least half the nation's asthma cases. If other things are responsible for half (or more than half) of the nation's asthma cases, then banning MTC will not have the desired effect of reducing asthma rates by half.

(B) While it might seem unwise for the government to ban products that are necessary for American prosperity, this consideration is outside the scope of the argument. The conclusion concerns whether a ban on MTC would be able to halve the nation's asthma rate. Nothing about the effect on prosperity must be assumed for that conclusion to follow.

(C) The fact that asthma has reached epidemic proportions might give the government a motive to ban asthma-causing substances such as MTC. However, the conclusion is not concerned with the government's motivation. That asthma has reached epidemic proportions does not have to be assumed for the conclusion to follow.

(D) This statement may be true, but it is irrelevant because the government's plan does not involve exercise or nutrition.

(E) The government's plan does not rely on the truth of this statement, because the plan does not target other possible causes of asthma. The conclusion assumes that MTC is responsible for at least half of asthma cases, while not addressing other possible causes at all.

3. Be A Good Driver

Traffic Safety Expert: In order to achieve a substantial reduction in the extremely high number of car accidents in our country, we should implement a radical new safe driving plan. Seat belts and air bags would be eliminated from the driver's side of all automobiles to provide the driver with the strongest possible incentive to drive safely. Further, an electroshock system would administer shocks to the driver if he or she exceeds the speed limit or engages in other unsafe driving practices.

In declaring that the radical new safe driving plan will help to reduce accident rates, the author assumes which of the following?

(A) Some car accidents are caused, at least partially, by unforeseen conditions that occur naturally, such as flash floods.

(B) Accidents in which one or both participants exceed 60 miles per hour account for a majority of all fatal car accidents.

(C) A significant number of accidents are the result of negligence or other unsafe driving practices on the part of the driver.

(D) To alleviate safety concerns, citizens should be allowed to reinstall their drivers' side seat belts and air bags at their own expense.

(E) If not implemented properly, electroshock systems can cause heart attacks and other health problems.

The correct answer choice fills in a **_FEASIBILITY OF A PREMISE_**.

The argument outlines a proposal for the country to reduce by a substantial amount the number of car accidents via a new safe driving plan. The plan would remove safety features on the driver's side of the vehicle, presumably so that the driver would be very likely to be injured if he or she is in an accident. In addition, the driver would receive shocks if he or she engaged in unsafe driving behavior, presumably to train him or her not to engage in such practices. The author assumes that a substantial number of accidents are due to driver error or could be avoided with a change in driver behavior. The author also assumes that the electroshock system will not itself cause a substantial number of accidents, or health problems that could lead to accidents.

(A) It is likely true that some accidents are the result of unforeseen conditions, such as a natural disaster. Such an assumption, however, does not negate the idea that some car accidents are due to driver error, or that forcing drivers to drive more safely will help to reduce the incidence of car accidents.

(B) This may very well be true, but the argument does not propose that the country lower speed limits in order to reduce the number of accidents. Further, the argument does mention that drivers would receive a shock for exceeding the speed limit, but it does not claim a majority of fatal car accidents involve speeding.

(C) **CORRECT.** The author claims that the new plan will result in a **substantial reduction** in the number of car accidents. For this to be true, the author must assume that a significant number of those accidents are a direct result of driver behavior and could be prevented via safer driving habits.

(D) Many citizens in the country in question may agree with this opinion, but the opinion has no bearing on whether the author's plan will result in the author's goal: a reduction in the number of car accidents. In fact, if enough people were to reinstall their own safety equipment, the plan would no longer be valid.

(E) This choice is the result of faulty logic. If the shock system that is meant to train people to be better drivers can cause immediate and severe health problems, this is not likely to be very helpful in reducing the incidence of car accidents. If anything, the author must be assuming that the system would be largely, if not entirely, safe.

4. Genetics

Two genes, BRCA1 and BRCA2, are linked to hereditary breast cancer. Therefore, in order to decrease the annual number of mammogram tests administered across a population and to more accurately assess a woman's individual risk of breast cancer, all women should be tested for these genes.

Which of the following is an assumption on which the argument depends?

(A) Some of the women who are tested for the two genes will subsequently undergo mammograms on a less frequent basis than they used to.
(B) The majority of breast cancer patients have no family history of the disease.
(C) Researchers may have identified a third breast cancer gene that is linked with hereditary breast cancer.
(D) Women who have these genes have an 80 percent chance of getting breast cancer, while women who do not have these genes have only a 10 percent chance of getting breast cancer.
(E) The presence of BRCA1 and BRCA2 can explain up to 50 percent of hereditary cases.

The correct answer choice establishes the **FEASIBILITY OF A PREMISE**.

This argument states that BRCA1 and BRCA2 are connected to hereditary breast cancer. It then concludes that all women should be tested for these genes in order to reduce the number of mammograms given annually and to more accurately determine their individual risk of breast cancer. This argument depends on the assumption that BRCA1 and BRCA2 are the primary genes that cause hereditary breast cancer, and also that at least some of the women who are tested will, in some way, reduce the frequency at which they undergo mammograms.

(A) CORRECT. As stated above, the author's position hinges on the assumption that at least some women will undergo fewer mammograms after being tested for the breast cancer-causing genes.

(B) It is not necessary to the argument that the majority of breast cancer patients have no family history of the disease. If anything, this choice could weaken the argument by implying that perhaps too few women carry the genes to make the testing worthwhile.

(C) The possible identification of a third breast cancer gene that is linked to hereditary breast cancer is irrelevant to this argument. The conclusion concerns testing for the two identified genes; the third gene is not part of the equation.

(D) While these statistics given might provide a strong incentive to encourage women to be tested, the given conclusion does not address whether the women will get breast cancer or even what they should do if they do have the genes. Rather, the conclusion asserts that all women should merely be tested for the two reasons given in the argument.

(E) This choice is an example of "switching terms." The two genes can explain up to 50% of hereditary cases. What portion of ALL cases is made up of hereditary cases? That information is not given. If hereditary cases make up 99% of all cases, then this choice might support the idea that being tested for the two genes would allow women to more accurately determine their risk. If hereditary cases make up 1% of all cases, then this choice would not support the idea that being tested for the two genes would allow women to more accurately determine risk. The choice is trying to muddle the issue by switching terms in an effort to get us to conclude something we cannot actually conclude.

5. Intercontinental Bank

Editorial: The Intercontinental Bank should reallocate the voting shares of its members in order to more effectively shape global economic policy. For example, China comprises about 15 percent of the world's gross domestic product but has only a 3 percent voting share, whereas Belgium, with less than 1 percent of the global economy, has a 2 percent share.

Which of the following is an assumption upon which the editorial's authors depend in suggesting a way to more effectively shape global economic policy?

(A) The United States has a larger voting share of the Intercontinental Bank than does China or Belgium.
(B) The specific allocation of voting shares factors into the Intercontinental Bank's effectiveness in shaping global economic policy.
(C) Only voting shares that are precisely proportional to each country's contribution to the global economy are appropriate for the Intercontinental Bank.
(D) The Intercontinental Bank is necessary to the maintenance of a prosperous global economy.
(E) As one of the fastest growing economies, China should have a larger voting share in the Intercontinental Bank.

The correct answer choice establishes the **FEASIBILITY OF A PREMISE**.

The Editorial states that a reallocation of the voting shares of the Intercontinental Bank is desirable in order for the Bank to more effectively shape global economic policy. Evidence is then presented that the voting shares of two countries, China and Belgium, are not in proportion to their contributions to the global economy. The argument does not actually present any evidence that the efficacy of the Intercontinental Bank will improve if voting shares are reallocated; this must be assumed in order to support the conclusion.

(A) There is no mention of the United States in the argument, and the conclusion does not hinge on the proportion of US shares relative to China's shares or Belgium's shares.

(B) CORRECT. The Editorial argues for a reallocation of voting shares in order for the Intercontinental Bank to more effectively shape global economic policy. This assumes that the way in which the Intercontinental Bank allocates shares is a factor in the Bank's ability to shape that policy.

(C) The way in which the evidence is presented does seem to imply that the Editorial might recommend a reallocation of voting shares that more closely reflects contributions to the global economy. However, there is no indication that the reallocation must be "precisely proportional" in order to be "appropriate." This answer choice is too extreme in its language.

(D) This may be true, but the given conclusion concerns how, or whether, the allocation of shares affects the Bank's effectiveness in shaping economic policy. An organization could help shape global economic policy without being vital to the proper functioning of the world economy.

(E) Though it could be true that the Editorial author would believe China should have a larger share, such a belief is not necessary to the conclusion. The conclusion merely states that a "reallocation" is necessary in order for the Bank to shape economic policy more effectively. The argument provides some statistics, but no specific recommendations as to how that reallocation should be carried out.

6. Fresh Start

Advertisement: According to a recent research study, daily use of Fresh Start, a new toothpaste, reduces the risk of developing dental cavities by over 20 percent. In addition, as a result of a new formula, the use of Fresh Start results in whiter, healthier-looking teeth. Clearly, Fresh Start not only gives your teeth a beautiful look but also provides the most reliable protection against dental cavities.

Which of the following is an assumption in the argument above?

(A) No other toothpaste provides more reliable protection against dental cavities.
(B) Fresh Start's formula does a better job of whitening teeth than do competitors' formulas.
(C) People are just as interested in having beautiful teeth as they are in having healthy teeth.
(D) Fresh Start also prevents other dental disorders, such as gingivitis.
(E) Reliable protection against dental cavities, combined with excellent aesthetic properties, is likely to make Fresh Start a popular toothpaste on the market.

*The correct answer choice eliminates an **ALTERNATE PATH TO THE SAME END.***

The conclusion of the argument is that Fresh Start not only gives your teeth a beautiful look but also provides the most reliable protection against dental cavities. Note the strong language *most reliable*, as this indicates that there is no other, better protection available against dental cavities.

ManhattanGMAT Prep
the new standard

(A) CORRECT. Since the argument singles out Fresh Start as the most reliable protection against dental cavities, the author must assume that no other toothpaste provides stronger protection against cavities. Otherwise, the conclusion of the argument is inaccurate.

(B) A premise states that Fresh Start's new formula results in *whiter, healthier-looking teeth*, but the argument does not tell us compared to what? The comparison could be to competitors' results, but it could also be to Fresh Start's old formula. Further, the conclusion only states that using Fresh Start will give teeth "a beautiful look." It does not conclude that using Fresh Start results in whiter teeth than does any other toothpaste.

(C) The conclusion does not make a distinction between customers' relative interest in beautiful teeth versus healthy teeth. This choice is therefore irrelevant.

(D) Since the advertisement focuses only on dental cavities, discussion of other dental disorders is beyond the scope of the argument.

(E) While the statement in this answer choice is quite plausible, this information does not have to be assumed, since the issue of popularity is beyond the scope of this argument.

7. Exchange Student

> Student Advisor: One of our exchange students faced multiple arguments with her parents over the course of the past year. Not surprisingly, her grade point average (GPA) over the same period showed a steep decline. This is just one example of a general truth: problematic family relationships can cause significant academic difficulties for our students.
>
> Which of the following is an assumption underlying the general truism claimed by the Student Advisor?
>
> (A) Last year, the exchange student reduced the amount of time spent on academic work, resulting in a lower GPA.
> (B) The decline in the GPA of the exchange student was not the reason for the student's arguments with her parents.
> (C) School GPA is an accurate measure of a student's intellectual ability.
> (D) If proper measures are not taken, the decline in the student's academic performance may become irreversible.
> (E) Fluctuations in academic performance are typical for many students.

*The correct answer choice eliminates an **ALTERNATE MODEL OF CAUSATION**.*

In this argument, the student advisor cites two correlated events that happened last year: (1) a series of arguments between the student and her parents and (2) a decline in her GPA. Using this evidence, the advisor concludes that problematic family relationships cause academic problems. However, to claim one causal relationship (that the arguments caused the decline in GPA), we need to exclude other possible causal relationships. For example, we need to assume that the reverse is not true: the decline in the GPA did not lead to the arguments between the student and her parents.

(A) There could have been many reasons for the decline in the student's GPA, such as poor concentration or less time spent studying, but any one potential cause is not absolutely necessary to assume. Further, the conclusion here addresses a causal relationship between the arguments and the decline in GPA; this choice does not address the given conclusion.

(B) CORRECT. This assumption correctly eliminates the alternate model of causation, demonstrating that the decline in the GPA did not cause the arguments between the student and her parents.

(C) The question of whether the GPA accurately measures a student's intellectual ability is beyond the scope of this argument. The conclusion does not make any claims about students' intellectual ability.

(D) This may be true, but the conclusion does not make any claims about the permanency or reversibility of the decline in GPA. The conclusion is about the cause of the decline; not what might happen after the decline occurs.

(E) Again, this may be true but, the conclusion does not make any claims about the frequency with which *many students* experience fluctuations in performance. It merely concludes that problematic relationships cause academic problems.

8. Oil and Ethanol

Country B's oil production is not sufficient to meet its domestic demand. In order to sharply reduce its dependence on foreign sources of oil, Country B recently embarked on a program requiring all of its automobiles to run on ethanol in addition to gasoline. Combined with its oil production, Country B produces enough ethanol from agricultural by-products to meet its current demand for energy.

Which of the following must be assumed in order to conclude that Country B will succeed in its plan to reduce its dependence on foreign oil?

(A) Electric power is not a superior alternative to ethanol in supplementing automobile gasoline consumption.
(B) In Country B, domestic production of ethanol is increasing more quickly than domestic oil production.
(C) Ethanol is suitable for the heating of homes and other applications aside from automobiles.
(D) In Country B, gasoline consumption is not increasing at a substantially higher rate than domestic oil and ethanol production.
(E) Ethanol is as efficient as gasoline in terms of mileage per gallon when used as fuel for automobiles.

The correct answer choice fills in a **LOGIC GAP**.

The argument concludes that the program will sharply reduce Country B's reliance upon foreign oil. As evidence, it states that Country B's oil production, combined with its ethanol production, is enough to meet Country B's current energy demands. However, this argument assumes either that Country B's energy demands will not increase beyond current levels or that the country will be able to produce additional oil and ethanol to meet any growth in demand. The correct answer choice will address this assumption.

(A) The argument does not mention electric power, nor does it claim that ethanol is superior to all other alternatives. The conclusion concerns only the claim that Country B can reduce its dependence on foreign oil via its own ethanol and oil production.

(B) The argument does not make a distinction between the amount of ethanol versus oil production, nor does it make a distinction about the rate of increase in production of either energy source. The claim simply says that the two sources combined are expected to substitute for the foreign oil.

(C) It is not necessary to the argument that ethanol be suitable for other applications for which oil is used. The conclusion asserts only that Country B will be able to reduce its dependence on foreign oil if it uses ethanol, in addition to oil, to power automobiles.

(D) **CORRECT.** The argument provides evidence that the domestic production of oil and ethanol are sufficient to meet current demand. However, if gasoline consumption were to increase at a substantially higher rate than oil and ethanol production, then domestic production would no longer meet domestic demand, and this specific program would not reduce Country B's reliance on foreign oil specifically by substituting domestic.

(E) It is not absolutely necessary to the argument that ethanol be as efficient, on a mile per gallon basis, as gasoline. The program could still reduce oil imports even if ethanol were not as efficient as gasoline.

9. Housing Insanity

An industry analyst asserted in his recent report that the relative scarcity of housing in a particular market leads to larger than normal increases in price. During the late 1990s, according to the analyst's report, occupancy rates—a measure of the percentage of housing occupied at a given time—in crowded urban markets such as New York and San Francisco hovered around 99.5%. During the same period, housing prices increased by as much as 100% per year, compared to more normal past increases in the range of 5% to 15% per year.

Which of the following is an assumption that supports the analyst's assertion?

(A) In the housing market, there generally must be at least five buyers per seller in order to cause larger than normal increases in price.

(B) Increases in demand often reflect an influx of new buyers into the marketplace or an unusual increase in buying power on the part of the customer.

(C) The U.S. housing market showed a larger than average increase in the 1990s across the country, not just in crowded urban areas.

(D) Price increases do not cause people to withhold their houses from the market in the hopes that prices will increase even further in the future.

(E) A significant rise in housing prices in a specific area may cause some potential buyers to relocate to other, less pricey areas.

*The correct answer choice eliminates an **ALTERNATE MODEL OF CAUSATION**.*

The analyst claims that, in the housing market, scarcity causes larger than normal price increases. The remaining premises are all facts that do not appear to have any logic gaps or other problems. The premises, however, represent only a correlation, not a cause–effect relationship: during a certain time period, occupancy rates were high and prices increased a great deal. The analyst claims that scarcity causes the price increase, but the reverse could also be true: the price increase could cause the scarcity. Perhaps people wait to sell because they think the market will continue to rise, or perhaps people will not sell their own property because they would then have to pay inflated prices for a new property. In order to conclude that scarcity causes prices to rise, the analyst must assume that the "reverse" causation does *not* occur.

(A) This generally addresses the scarcity idea discussed in the the argument but, if it were proved untrue, it would not damage the argument, because the argument does not claim a particular level of scarcity required to result in larger than normal price increases.

(B) This choice speculates on the causes of an increase in demand, but the argument does not make a claim on this issue; rather it claims that scarcity specifically leads to price increases. If this were not true, it would not affect the argument in either a positive or a negative way.

(C) Although this may be true in the real world, it does not address the claim made by the argument that scarcity causes the price increase. It just presents an additional, general fact. If anything, it might weaken the argument, if there were larger than normal price increases in areas were there was no scarcity of housing.

(D) **CORRECT.** This choice denies the reverse causation possibility: greater than normal price increases do not lead to increased scarcity. In order to make his claim, the analyst must assume this possible causation does not occur; if this possibility were not denied, the argument would be damaged.

(E) This choice indicates that a rise in prices can cause certain people to opt for other, less expensive areas. This is a mitigating factor that could keep prices from rising too high; it is not an assumption that is helpful to the argument.

10. Movie Money

Studio executives carefully examine how a film performs on its opening weekend in order to determine whether—and how—to invest more in that film. Many decisions, such as increasing the number of screens that show the film and expanding the marketing campaign, are best made after reactions can be gathered from audiences who actually purchased tickets. Therefore, to maximize returns on their marketing investments, studios should initially release all their films on a small number of screens and with a limited advertising campaign.

The plan to maximize returns by initially releasing films on only a small number of screens and limiting advertising depends upon which of the following assumptions?

(A) Large marketing investments made before the opening weekend never eventually yield greater profits than small initial marketing investments.
(B) New advertising techniques, such as Web-based viral marketing, have not substantially reduced the average marketing costs for films.
(C) A film's prior performance in noncommercial settings, such as festivals, is not well correlated with how the general public tends to react to that film.
(D) Across the movie industry, marketing investments do not influence the eventual financial returns of films in predictable ways.
(E) How a film performs during its opening weekend is a strong indicator of the film's financial performance over its lifetime.

*The correct answer choice eliminates an **ALTERNATE PATH TO THE SAME END**.*

According to the argument, all films should be released conservatively, in order to obtain the greatest return on marketing investments. The rationale given is that audience reactions can only be properly gathered and interpreted after the opening weekend; these reactions then serve as the basis for marketing decisions such as expanding the film's release. However, the argument ignores other possible means to achieve the stated goal of maximum returns on marketing investments. Specifically, the argument overlooks the impact of marketing decisions that are made before opening weekend, such as the initial number of screens or the initial size of the advertising campaign; such decisions could influence the results of the opening weekend. In fact, investing a great deal in marketing before a film opens might be the best way to generate profits, as in the case of blockbusters or of films predicted to collapse after the opening weekend. Note that several of the incorrect answers reinforce a conservative attitude toward releasing a film, but none of them are critical to the validity of the conclusion, and thus none are assumptions upon which the conclusion depends.

(A) CORRECT. In order to conclude that all films should have limited releases, it must not be possible for large pre-release marketing spending to lead to the best returns on investment, no matter what film is considered. Also, check the LEN: large marketing investments made before the opening weekend could eventually yield greater profits than small initial marketing investments. The author's conclusion would fall apart if this were true.

(B) If marketing costs fell, then releasing films might be less risky. However, the conclusion here is concerned with how to maximize profits. This choice does not address whether a conservative release plan is the best method to maximize profits.

(C) This is a tempting choice. A premise in the argument says that reactions from commercial audiences are the most useful indicators in making marketing decisions. Try the LEN strategy: performance in non-commercial settings is at least somewhat correlated with how the general public tends to react. Does this destroy the conclusion? No. The non-commercial audience reactions could be decently correlated without being the most useful type of audience reaction.

(D) The author claims that limited releases are the best means to maximize returns on marketing investments. In other words, the author is predicting something about the expected return on a marketing investment. At the same time, the author's conclusion does not logically depend on whether marketing investments have predictable effects or not.

(E) The opening weekend's results may be a strong indicator of future performance, but that does not allow us to conclude that the given plan will always result in the best financial returns on a marketing investment. There may be other, better indicators of future performance.

REAL GMAT PROBLEMS

Now that you have completed your study of FIND THE ASSUMPTION questions, you may also test your skills on passages that have actually appeared on real GMAT exams over the past several years.

The problem set below is composed of Critical Reasoning passages from two books published by GMAC (Graduate Management Admission Council):

The Official Guide for GMAT Review, 11th Edition (pages 32–38 & 468–504)
The Official Guide for GMAT Verbal Review (pages 116–142)

Continue to diagram each argument, but this time, you should answer each question. Also, try to identify which type of assumption is represented by the correct answer.

<u>Note</u>: Problem numbers preceded by "D" refer to questions in the Diagnostic Test chapter of *The Official Guide for GMAT Review, 11th Edition* (pages 32–38).

Find the Assumption
    11th Edition: 2, 14, 25, 32, 47, 50, 52, 59, 77, 80, 81, 89, 92, 96, 97, 105, 109, 110, D28
    Verbal Review: 7, 13, 34, 45, 51, 56, 63, 67, 75

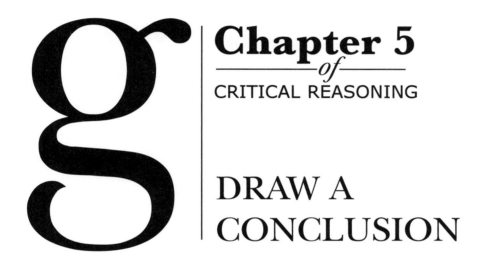

Chapter 5
of
CRITICAL REASONING

DRAW A
CONCLUSION

In This Chapter . . .

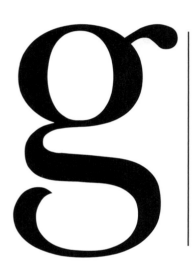

- Draw a Conclusion Overview
- Stay Close to the Premises
- Use Real Numbers
- Make an Inference
- Wrong Answer Choice Types

DRAW A CONCLUSION

Draw a Conclusion questions ask you to conclude something from a set of given premises. The question stem may take different forms:

> If the statements above are true, which of the following must be true?

> Which of the following conclusions is best supported by the information above?

When the GMAT provides a conclusion in an argument, that conclusion is an arguable statement, or claim, that is <u>partially</u> supported by the premises of the argument. By contrast, if you are asked to DRAW a conclusion (and find that conclusion in the answer choices), that conclusion <u>must be true</u> as a result of only the given premises. The conclusion should not require you to make any additional assumptions at all, even tiny ones. The correct answer to a Draw a Conclusion question is NOT a claim or an arguable statement.

Stay Close to the Premises

The conclusion you select should necessarily be supported by at least some of the premises. The conclusion does <u>not</u> need to address all of the premises. A correct answer might simply restate one or more of the premises, often using synonyms. Alternatively, a correct answer might be a mathematical or logical deduction.

Consider the following example:

> In certain congested urban areas, commuters who use public transportation options such as trains and subways spend approximately 25 percent less time in transit, on average, to reach their destinations than commuters who opt instead to take cars to their destinations. Even individuals who drive their entire commute in carpool lanes, which are typically the least congested sections of roadways, still spend more time, on average, than commuters who use trains and subways.

> The statements above, if true, best support which of the following assertions about commuting in the congested urban areas mentioned above?

> (A) Waiting in traffic accounts for approximately 25 percent of the commuting time for individuals who drive to their destinations.
> (B) Walking between a subway or train station and one's final destination does not, on average, take longer than walking between one's car and one's final destination.
> (C) Using carpool lanes does not, on average, reduce driving time by more than 25 percent.
> (D) Individuals who commute via public buses spend approximately 25 percent more time in transit than those who commute using public trains or subways.
> (E) Subways and trains are available in the majority of congested urban areas.

Draw a conclusion that does not require any assumptions or information beyond the given premises.

DRAW A CONCLUSION

In Draw a Conclusion questions, the <u>entire body</u> of the argument represents premises. A T-diagram for the above argument might look like this:

Cong urb area, comm on pblc trans take 25% < time (avg) than ppl who drive
Carpool lanes usly least cong
EVEN SO Carpool lanes still take ↑ time (avg) than pblc trans

Look for an answer choice that simply restates information given in the passage.

We are looking for a conclusion that must be true according to this information.

Answer choice (**A**) states that waiting in traffic accounts for 25 percent of the commuting time for drivers. However, nothing in the passage alludes to waiting in traffic. This *may* be a reason why driving takes longer than using public transportation, but it does not *have* to be true.

Answer choice (**B**) makes a claim about particular segments of the different commutes. However, the passage never mentions which segments of the commute provide the speed advantage to public transportation. It is certainly possible that walking to the subway takes longer than walking to one's car and that the speed advantage is realized from some other segment of the commute.

Answer choice (**C**) does not make much of a claim at all. It simply restates the information given in the passage. If taking subways or trains reduce one's commute time, on average, by 25 percent, and if using carpool lanes does not eliminate the speed advantage of public transportation, then it follows that carpool lanes do not reduce driving time by more than 25 percent. Thus, answer choice (**C**) is correct.

Answer choice (**D**) introduces a claim about public buses, which are never mentioned in the passage. While it is possible that public buses are similar to cars in terms of commuting time, it is certainly not necessary and does not follow from any information given.

Answer choice (**E**) makes a claim about *the majority* of congested urban areas. The premises, on the other hand, reference only *certain* congested urban areas. Thus, this answer choice uses an overly broad term that goes beyond the scope of the passage. It does not have to be true that a majority has these specific types of public transport.

Notice that the correct answer, (**C**), did NOT weave together all the premises into a grand plan. The correct conclusion that you can draw from a set of premises must always be a provable fact. Thus, it will generally restate a premise, sometimes in a mathematically equivalent way. The mathematical equivalence provides a slight disguise for the truth. For instance, the premise *More precipitation falls on the Sahara than on Antarctica* can be restated as *Less precipitation falls on Antarctica than on the Sahara.*

Use Real Numbers

If an argument involves percentages, it can be helpful to use concrete, real numbers.

We can revisit the previous example. The correct answer, choice **(C)** states *Using carpool lanes does not, on average, reduce driving time by more than 25 percent.*

Imagine that it takes 40 minutes, on average, to commute via car. We know from the premises that it takes 25 percent less time to commute via subway or train, equal to a 10 minute reduction (25 percent of 40 is 10). Thus, the average commute using public transportation is 30 minutes. We also know from the premises that those who drive in carpool lanes still take longer than 30 minutes.

Therefore, it is clear from the premises that the carpool lanes do not reduce drive time by more than 10 minutes (or 25 percent). This is exactly what answer choice **(C)** states.

Inference, assertion, prediction and claim are all synonyms for conclusion.

Make an Inference

GMAT conclusions may also be labeled "Inferences." For example, a question may ask:

Which of the following can be properly inferred from the passage?

The word *inference* is essentially a synonym for *conclusion*. As such, an inference should also follow <u>directly</u> from the premises; it should be <u>unequivocally true</u> according to those premises.

Consider this example:

Curbing government spending has been demonstrated to raise the value of a country's currency over time. However, many economists no longer recommend this policy. A currency of lesser value causes a country's exports to be more competitive in the international market, encouraging domestic industries and making the economy more attractive to foreign investment.

The statements above most strongly support which of the following inferences?

(A) Limited government spending can also lead to a reduction in the national deficit.
(B) Curbing government spending can make a country's exports less competitive.
(C) Many economists now recommend higher levels of government spending.
(D) An increase in the value of a currency will result in reduced government spending.
(E) Competitive exports indicate a weak currency.

DRAW A CONCLUSION

A T-diagram for the above argument might look like this:

↓ gov spend → ↑ value of $$
BUT econ no longer rec this
$ of ↓ value → more comp exports, better biz, better for foreign invest

Correct conclusions must be true, according to the information in the premises.

The correct answer choice should be an inarguable statement that follows directly from the premises.

Answer choice **(A)** may be generally plausible, but the given premises do not mention the national deficit. This answer choice does not <u>have</u> to be true as a result of the information given in the argument. You must refrain from bringing any external facts/premises that you may know into the argument.

Answer choice **(C)** might also be generally plausible, but **(C)**, too, requires an additional step from the premises. The fact that economists no longer recommend <u>reduced</u> government spending does not necessarily mean that many economists now recommend <u>increased</u> spending. It is possible that they recommend neutral spending levels.

Both answer choices **(D)** and **(E)** employ faulty logic. It may be true that reduced government spending will increase a currency's value, but we do not know whether the reverse is true. Increasing a currency's value does not necessarily have to result in reduced government spending. Similarly, though a weak currency will make exports more competitive, competitive exports do not necessarily indicate a weak currency; exports may be competitive on some other grounds (e.g. exceptional quality).

Answer choice **(B)** is correct as it follows directly from the premises. According to the argument, curbing government spending can raise a currency's value. A weaker currency makes a country's exports more competitive. A stronger currency, then, would make a country's exports less competitive than they would have been with a weaker currency. Thus, curbing government spending can make a country's exports less competitive.

Notice that the word *can* makes this answer choice a very limited claim. This choice does not state that curbing government spending <u>will</u> make a country's exports less competitive. All we are told is that this outcome is a possibility, one which follows directly from the premises. Answer choice **(B)** is the correct answer.

Wrong Answer Choice Types

As we discussed in the Find the Assumption chapter, knowing common categories of wrong answers can help you with the process of elimination. Again, use this classification if you are otherwise stuck.

The key to a correct answer on a Draw a Conclusion question is to find an answer choice which *must* be true as a result of <u>some</u> or <u>all</u> of the information given in the argument.

Take a look again at a previous sample argument:

> Curbing government spending has been demonstrated to raise the value of a country's currency over time. However, many economists no longer recommend this policy. A currency of lesser value causes a country's exports to be more competitive in the international market, encouraging domestic industries and making the economy more attractive to foreign investment.

The most common wrong answer type is called "Out of Scope." However, the way in which Draw a Conclusion answers are out of scope is somewhat different from the way in which Find The Assumption answers are out of scope. (After all, the "No Tie to the Conclusion" type requires the argument to have a conclusion already.)

A. Out Of Scope

For Draw a Conclusion questions, "Out of Scope" answers require you to assume at least one piece of information not *explicitly* presented in the argument. For example, answer choices (**A**) and (**C**) for the above argument both go beyond the scope of the argument:

> (A) Limited government spending can also lead to a reduction in the national deficit.

> (C) Many economists now recommend higher levels of government spending.

Answer choice (**A**) may be obviously out of scope because this choice mentions *the national deficit*, which is not mentioned anywhere in the argument. Answer choice (**C**), on the other hand, may be much more tempting because it addresses concepts that were mentioned in the argument. How do we recognize and avoid such tempting wrong answers?

A subset of Out of Scope answers will contain information that seems "Real-World Plausible." In other words, this information is very plausible, or likely to be true in the real world. The answer may even contain what people would reasonably surmise to be true in an article or conversation about the general topic. The Draw a Conclusion question type, however, requires us to find something that <u>must</u> be true according to the given premises, not something that <u>could</u> be true or merely sounds reasonable. Often people are surprised at how simple the conclusions are—the correct answer will be very closely tied to the premises. Another choice may seem reasonable in the real world, but you are not allowed to go outside the premises given. If you cannot say that the premises prove an answer choice to be true, eliminate that answer choice. Do not bring external knowledge into the picture on Draw a Conclusion questions.

Practice categorizing incorrect answer choice types so that you can quickly identify them on test day.

B. Wrong Direction and **C. Switching Terms**

We encountered these other common types of wrong answers in the Find the Assumption chapter. A "Wrong Direction" answer might provide a conclusion that is the opposite of what the argument says. The reason why such a conclusion would be proposed is that under exam pressure, you might not notice the reversal. For example, a "Wrong Direction" answer choice for the argument above could read as follows:

> Curbing government spending can make a country's exports more competitive.

This statement actually asserts the opposite of what the premises together imply.

Alternatively, the answer might "switch terms" or otherwise propose faulty mathematical or logical reasoning. For example, a "Switching Terms" answer choice could read as follows:

> Government programs can make a country's exports less competitive.

Government programs and *curbing government spending* are not the same thing. Make sure that any substituted expressions are truly synonyms.

Likewise, we saw that answer choices **(D)** and **(E)** for the argument above switched causes and effects proposed by the premises:

> (D) An increase in the value of a currency will result in reduced government spending.
> (E) Competitive exports indicate a weak currency.

These answer choices use terms that are identical or nearly identical to those used in the premises. However, neither choice actually follows logically from those premises.

Problem Set

Use the skills you have just learned to answer the following Draw a Conclusion questions. Be sure to diagram each argument. Detailed answers and explanations follow this problem set.

1. Two Universities

Both enrollment and total tuition revenue at Brownsville University have increased during each of the last four years. During the same period of time, enrollment at Canterbury University has steadily decreased, while total tuition revenue has remained constant.

Which of the following assertions is best supported by the statements above?

(A) Brownsville University now collects more total tuition revenue than Canterbury University.
(B) Students regard higher tuition as an indicator of higher quality.
(C) The per-student tuition at Canterbury University has risen over the last four years.
(D) Within four years, enrollment at Brownsville University will likely exceed enrollment at Canterbury University.
(E) Canterbury University will likely continue to raise tuition to make up for lost revenue from declining enrollment.

2. Antarctic Meteorite

A detailed lab analysis of a meteorite recently discovered in Antarctica revealed that the meteorite has geological characteristics common to the planet Mars. To date, scientists have not found these characteristics anywhere other than on Mars. Using a technique called "acid-etching," scientists found that the meteorite contained fossilized remains of single-cell life forms.

The statements above, if true, best support which of the following as a conclusion?

(A) The fossilized remains indicate that life exists on Mars.
(B) The scientists have evidence to support a hypothesis that the meteorite came from Mars.
(C) The meteorite represents a substantial step forward in human knowledge of the development of life in the solar system.
(D) Undiscovered meteorites currently exist in Antarctica.
(E) "Acid-etching" is necessary to confirm the existence of fossilized remains in meteorites.

3. Miles Per Gallon

The average fuel efficiency of vehicles sold nationwide during the period 2000–2004 was 25 miles per gallon; the corresponding figure during the period 1995–1999 was 20 miles per gallon. The national average price of gasoline during the period 2000–2004 was $2 per gallon; the corresponding figure during the period 1995–1999 was $1.60 per gallon.

The statements above, if true, best support which of the following conclusions?

(A) The average fuel efficiency of vehicles sold nationwide should reach 30 miles per gallon for the period 2005–2009.
(B) The national average price of gasoline during 1997 was lower than the corresponding price during 2003.

(C) Rising gasoline prices lead consumers to purchase more fuel-efficient cars.

(D) Between the two described time periods, the national average fuel efficiency and the national average gasoline price both increased at roughly the same rate.

(E) Consumers spent more money on gasoline during the period 2000–2004 than during the period 1995–1999.

4. Pulverized Vase

Museum A will henceforth display only undamaged objects of proven authenticity. Doubts have been raised about the origins of a supposedly Mycenaean vase currently on display in the museum's antiquities wing. The only way to establish this vase's authenticity would be to pulverize it, then subject the dust to spectroscopic analysis.

The claims above, if true, most strongly support which of the following conclusions?

(A) Authentic Mycenaean vases are valuable and rare.

(B) Museum A has been beset with questions about the provenance of many of the items in its antiquities wing.

(C) The vase in question will no longer be displayed in Museum A.

(D) Spectroscopic analysis has revolutionized the forensic investigation of art forgery.

(E) Knowingly or not, many of the world's museums display some forgeries.

5. Military Alumni

Of all the high schools in the United States, Judd Academy is the one with the largest number of alumni serving in the Air Force. Knoxworth High School, however, is the school with the most graduates serving in the military as a whole, including the Army, Navy, Air Force, Marines, and Coast Guard.

Which of the following, if true, is most clearly supported by the statements above?

(A) Knoxworth is the most patriotic town in the nation.

(B) Judd Academy has fewer graduates serving in the Navy than does Knoxworth High School.

(C) Judd Academy has a higher percentage of alumni serving in the Air Force than does Knoxworth High School.

(D) Some graduates of Knoxworth High School are serving in the military but not in the Air Force.

(E) Knoxworth High School is the school with the second-highest number of alumni serving in the Air Force.

6. Network Television

In 1984, network television commercials accounted for 80% of all network and non-network television advertising revenue. In 2004, that figure was 60%. During that same period, operating costs for the networks remained steady, and in 2004 every major network announced record-setting profits.

The information above, if true, supports which of the following conclusions?

(A) Between 1984 and 2004, the number of homes with access to non-network television channels increased by more than 20%.

*Manhattan*GMAT*Prep

the new standard

(B) Teenagers comprise a growing proportion of television viewers, and teenagers prefer to watch non-network television shows.

(C) The amount of advertising revenue earned from non-network television commercials in 2004 was greater than the amount of revenue earned by network television commercials in 1984.

(D) Between 1984 and 2004, advertising revenue earned from non-network television commercials grew at a faster rate than revenue earned from network television commercials.

(E) Soon advertising revenue from non-network television commercials will surpass revenue from network television commercials.

7. Stem Cell Research

Government restrictions have severely limited the amount of stem cell research American companies can conduct. Because of these restrictions, many American scientists who specialize in the field of stem cell research have signed long term contracts to work for foreign companies. Recently, Congress has proposed lifting all restrictions on stem cell research.

Which of the following statements can most properly be inferred from the information above?

(A) Some foreign companies that conduct stem cell research work under fewer restrictions than some American companies do.

(B) Because American scientists are under long-term contracts to foreign companies, there will be a significant influx of foreign professionals into the United States.

(C) In all parts of the world, stem cell research is dependent on the financial backing of local government.

(D) In the near future, American companies will no longer be at the forefront of stem cell research.

(E) If restrictions on stem cell research are lifted, many of the American scientists will break their contracts to return to American companies.

8. Gift Catalogue

Gift Catalogue Inc. sent seven custom-made gift packages last week. Last week, all of the shipments from Gift Catalogue Inc. that were sent out on Wednesday or later consisted entirely of non-custom-made gift packages. Gift Catalogue Inc. sent seven gift packages to Technocorp last week, at least two of which were custom-made gift packages.

If the statements in the passage above are true, which of the following must also be true about Gift Catalogue Inc.?

(A) At least one of the gift packages sent to Technocorp last week was not custom-made.

(B) At least one of the custom-made gift packages sent last week was not directed to Technocorp.

(C) The majority of the gift packages sent to Technocorp last week were sent on Wednesday or later.

(D) Some of the gift packages sent to Technocorp last week were sent on Tuesday or earlier.

(E) Technocorp received a higher proportion of the gift packages sent last week from Gift Catalogue Inc. than any other recipient.

9. Mutual Funds

Many managers of mutual funds proclaim that they have been able to generate consistently higher rates of return on their investments than the general stock market by buying shares of undervalued companies. Classical economic theory, however, proposes the "efficient capital markets hypothesis," which proposes that stock prices accurately reflect the value of the underlying investments, incorporating all information available to the public. If the efficient capital markets hypothesis is correct, then it should be expected that _____.

(A) mutual fund managers, in order to compete with each other, will bid up the prices of certain stocks beyond their true values
(B) mutual fund managers use insider information, an illegal practice, to generate higher rates of return than the general stock market
(C) stock prices will rise over time
(D) given public information alone, companies cannot reliably be labeled undervalued or overvalued relative to the general stock market
(E) some mutual fund managers are better than others at generating a higher rate of return on investments

10. Real Estate Prices

In the last year, real estate prices, such as those for houses and condominiums, have gone up an average of 7% in the city of Galway but only 2% in the town of Tuam. On the other hand, average rents for apartments have risen 8% in Tuam over the last year, but only 4% in Galway.

Which of the following is an inference that can be reasonably drawn from the premises given above?

(A) In the last year, the ratio of average apartment rents to average real estate prices has increased in Tuam but fallen in Galway.
(B) Tuam has experienced a greater shift in demand toward the rental market than Galway has.
(C) It has become easier for Galway real estate to be bought and sold, whereas it has become easier for Tuam real estate to be rented.
(D) The supply of rental apartment units has decreased more in Tuam than in Galway.
(E) The average amount spent on housing is higher in Galway than it is in Tuam.

1. Two Universities

> Both enrollment and total tuition revenue at Brownsville University have increased during each of the last four years. During the same period of time, enrollment at Canterbury University has steadily decreased, while total tuition revenue has remained constant.
>
> Which of the following assertions is best supported by the statements above?
>
> (A) Brownsville University now collects more total tuition revenue than Canterbury University.
> (B) Students regard higher tuition as an indicator of higher quality.
> (C) The per-student tuition at Canterbury University has risen over the last four years.
> (D) Within four years, enrollment at Brownsville University will likely exceed enrollment at Canterbury University.
> (E) Canterbury University will likely continue to raise tuition to make up for lost revenue from declining enrollment.

This paragraph discusses the different enrollment and tuition trends at two universities during the same period of time. Brownsville University has experienced growth in both areas, while Canterbury University has not. We should look for an answer choice that results directly from these trends, and be wary of answer choices that go beyond them.

(A) We have no information regarding the number of students enrolled at either college. We also do not know the tuition rates. Therefore, we have no basis to calculate the total revenue from tuition at either school.

(B) This choice may be tempting because more students are enrolling at Brownsville University each year, even as it increases tuition. However, the answer choice is only one of many possible explanations for these trends. The college may have constructed a new dormitory or received significant publicity from a successful athletic team. Nothing in the premises suggests that students connect the rising fees with higher quality.

(C) **CORRECT.** This answer choice accurately connects the premises about enrollment and tuition, stating a conclusion that can be logically proven. Canterbury University has had constant revenue despite steadily declining enrollment. Therefore, each individual student must be paying more tuition.

(D) Although Brownsville University's enrollment is rising while that of Canterbury University is falling, Canterbury University may have started with a much larger student body. We have no numerical information to indicate how many years it would take Brownsville to surpass Canterbury in enrollment. More importantly, the premises do not predict how many students will enroll at either school in the coming years. The trends may reverse themselves at any time.

(E) The argument does not suggest how Canterbury University will deal with its declining revenue. It may cut expenses, or seek revenue from other sources. The fact that tuition is the only revenue source mentioned in the argument does not mean that raising tuition is Canterbury University's only course of action.

2. Antarctic Meteorite

A detailed lab analysis of a meteorite recently discovered in Antarctica revealed that the meteorite has geological characteristics common to the planet Mars. To date, scientists have not found these characteristics anywhere other than on Mars. Using a technique called "acid-etching," scientists found that the meteorite contained fossilized remains of single-cell life forms.

The statements above, if true, best support which of the following as a conclusion?

(A) The fossilized remains indicate that life exists on Mars.
(B) The scientists have evidence to support a hypothesis that the meteorite came from Mars.
(C) The meteorite represents a substantial step forward in human knowledge of the development of life in the solar system.
(D) Undiscovered meteorites currently exist in Antarctica.
(E) "Acid-etching" is necessary to confirm the existence of fossilized remains in meteorites.

This argument states that the fossilized remains of single cell life forms were found in a meteorite with geological characteristics unique to Mars. We should seek to eliminate answer choices that go beyond the premises or are too extreme.

(A) This answer choice concludes too much by saying that there is presently life on Mars. This answer is too extreme to be supported by the argument. For example, it is possible that the fossils represent a form of life that has since died out on Mars.

(B) CORRECT. The passage states that the meteorites have geological characteristics currently only known to exist on the planet Mars.

(C) There is no indication that the meteorite has revealed any new information about the development of life in the solar system. It is possible that scientists had earlier identified fossilized remains from Mars or other sources.

(D) This choice is beyond the scope of the argument. While it is reasonable to assume that there may be more undiscovered meteorites in Antarctica, such an assumption does not have to follow from the information presented.

(E) The argument states that scientists used a technique called "acid-etching" to find that the meteorite contained the fossilized remains of single-cell organisms. However, it is possible that there are other techniques that could also determine the existence of fossilized remains.

3. Miles Per Gallon

The average fuel efficiency of vehicles sold nationwide during the period 2000–2004 was 25 miles per gallon; the corresponding figure during the period 1995–1999 was 20 miles per gallon. The national average price of gasoline during the period 2000–2004 was $2 per gallon; the corresponding figure during the period 1995–1999 was $1.60 per gallon.

ManhattanGMAT Prep
the new standard

The statements above, if true, best support which of the following conclusions?

(A) The average fuel efficiency of vehicles sold nationwide should reach 30 miles per gallon for the period 2005–2009.
(B) The national average price of gasoline during 1997 was lower than the corresponding price during 2003.
(C) Rising gasoline prices lead consumers to purchase more fuel-efficient cars.
(D) Between the two described time periods, the national average fuel efficiency and the national average gasoline price both increased at roughly the same rate.
(E) Consumers spent more money on gasoline during the period 2000–2004 than during the period 1995–1999.

The premises enumerate the increases in both fuel efficiency and gasoline prices over two consecutive five-year periods. We should look for a conclusion that derives directly and inevitably from these increases. Likewise, we should avoid statements that speculate about possible causes or consequences.

(A) This choice offers a future prediction: what might happen to the average fuel efficiency figure during the period 2005–2009. Future predictions might come true but they do not have to come true; this choice does not follow unequivocally from the given premises.

(B) The averages were taken over a five-year period. Prices may have fluctuated wildly during those years. The average price per gallon may have been $3 in 1997 and $1 in 1998. Average prices during a period do not indicate any floor or ceiling for a specific year within that period.

(C) Consumer behavior cannot be explained by one or two sets of data. Many factors may have influenced consumers' buying habits. Furthermore, this choice only refers to cars. The question provides data on the average fuel efficiency of vehicles sold nationwide. The gains in fuel efficiency may be largely due to sales of other types of vehicles, such as trucks.

(D)**CORRECT.** The statements clearly indicate that both fuel efficiency and gasoline price averages increased by 25% from the earlier period to the later one.

(E) Although the price per gallon increased, the argument provides no data about the number of gallons purchased in either period. Hence, we cannot be certain that consumers spent more money overall on gasoline, only that they paid more, on average, for each gallon.

4. Pulverized Vase

Museum A will henceforth display only undamaged objects of proven authenticity. Doubts have been raised about the origins of a supposedly Mycenaean vase currently on display in the museum's antiquities wing. The only way to establish this vase's authenticity would be to pulverize it, then subject the dust to spectroscopic analysis.

The claims above, if true, most strongly support which of the following conclusions?

(A) Authentic Mycenaean vases are valuable and rare.

(B) Museum A has been beset with questions about the provenance of many of the
items in its antiquities wing.
(C) The vase in question will no longer be displayed in Museum A.
(D) Spectroscopic analysis has revolutionized the forensic investigation of art forgery.
(E) Knowingly or not, many of the world's museums display some forgeries.

We are told that a supposedly Mycenaean vase is of unproven authenticity, and that the only way to
establish its authenticity would involve damaging it (specifically, pulverizing it). Since the museum
will henceforth display only undamaged objects of proven authenticity, we can conclude that the
museum can no longer display this vase. Either the vase remains intact but possibly inauthentic—in
which case, it cannot be shown—or it is pulverized, in which case it again cannot be shown.

(A) The argument never mentions the concepts of value or scarcity, so this answer choice is not
supported by the premises.

(B) We are simply told that one item in the antiquities wing is of doubtful origin. This does not
prove that questions have been raised about more than one of the items in the wing.

(C) CORRECT. The argument establishes that the museum cannot continue to both follow its new
rule and display this vase. Either the vase will be tested with spectroscopic analysis, in which
case there will no longer be a vase to display, or the vase will not be tested, in which case the
museum cannot continue to display the vase under its authenticity policy.

(D) The argument mentions a single instance, relating to one ancient vase, in which spectroscopic
analysis would be useful in investigating whether an art object is a forgery. This is not enough
evidence to warrant the extreme conclusion that spectroscopic analysis has *revolutionized* the
forensic investigation of art forgery.

(E) The argument tells us of one possible forgery in one museum. No information is given that
could justify the extreme conclusion that many of the world's museums display forgeries.

5. Military Alumni
Of all the high schools in the United States, Judd Academy is the one with the
largest number of alumni serving in the Air Force. Knoxworth High School, however, is the school with the most graduates serving in the military as a whole, including the Army, Navy, Air Force, Marines, and Coast Guard.

Which of the following, if true, is most clearly supported by the statements above?

(A) Knoxworth is the most patriotic town in the nation.
(B) Judd Academy has fewer graduates serving in the Navy than does Knoxworth
High School.
(C) Judd Academy has a higher percentage of alumni serving in the Air Force than
does Knoxworth High School.
(D) Some graduates of Knoxworth High School are serving in the military but not
in the Air Force.
(E) Knoxworth High School is the school with the second-highest number of alumni
serving in the Air Force.

the new standard

We know that there are more Judd alumni than Knoxworth alumni serving in the Air Force. We also know that there are more Knoxworth alumni than Judd alumni serving in the military. How can both of these statements be true? Only if there are enough Knoxworth alumni in non-Air Force parts of the military to give Knoxworth a higher total than Judd for alumni in the military. Therefore, we should look for an answer choice that makes a statement about the existence of (or perhaps the number of) Knoxworth alumni in non-Air Force parts of the military.

(A) The argument does not tell us why so many graduates of Knoxworth High School are serving in the military. Possibly the reason has to do with patriotism, but the argument does not give us this information. Another problem with this answer choice is that we do not know how representative the alumni of Knoxworth High School are of the Knoxworth community as a whole.

(B) It is true that the number of Judd alumni in non-Air Force military roles must be smaller than the number of Knoxworth alumni in non-Air Force military roles. However, it is still possible that Judd Academy has more alumni serving in the Navy than does Knoxworth High School. Perhaps, the number of Knoxworth alumni in the other military services (Army, Marines, and Coast Guard) more than make up for Judd Academy's numerical advantage with respect to Navy and Air Force alumni.

(C) The premises of this argument tell us about absolute numbers of alumni from each school serving in the military or Air Force. Without information about the total number of alumni from each school, we cannot compare the two schools' percentages of alumni serving in the Air Force.

(D) CORRECT. In order for there to be more Knoxworth alumni than Judd alumni in the military even though there are more Judd alumni than Knoxworth alumni in the Air Force, there must be some Knoxworth alumni serving in non-Air Force parts of the military.

(E) This does not need to be true. For all we know, Knoxworth might have no alumni serving in the Air Force. Its status as the school with the most graduates serving in the military might only result from the presence of a very large number of alumni in non-Air Force military roles.

6. Network Television

In 1984, network television commercials accounted for 80% of all network and non-network television advertising revenue. In 2004, that figure was 60%. During that same period, operating costs for the networks remained steady, and in 2004 every major network announced record-setting profits.

The information above, if true, supports which of the following conclusions?

(A) Between 1984 and 2004, the number of homes with access to non-network television channels increased by more than 20%.

(B) Teenagers comprise a growing proportion of television viewers, and teenagers prefer to watch non-network television shows.

(C) The amount of advertising revenue earned from non-network television commercials in 2004 was greater than the amount of revenue earned by network television commercials in 1984.

(D) Between 1984 and 2004, advertising revenue earned from non-network television commercials grew at a faster rate than revenue earned from network television commercials.

(E) Soon advertising revenue from non-network television commercials will surpass revenue from network television commercials.

In the argument above, it is important to recognize that revenue from network television commercials is not necessarily going down; rather, what is going down is its proportion relative to non-network television advertising revenue. In fact, because costs have remained steady and profits have increased, we can conclude that total revenue for networks has gone up.

(A) The argument concerns advertising revenue; we are given no information about access to non-network television. While it can be argued that access is indirectly related to revenue, we are not given any information that allows us to draw a direct connection between the two.

(B) The argument did not distinguish the viewers by age group, and we know of nothing that directly connects the changes in advertising revenue with specific categories of viewers.

(C) Since the argument contains information only about percentages, or relative amounts, we cannot ascertain actual dollar amounts.

(D) CORRECT. If profit grew, and costs remained steady, we know that revenues from network television commercials must have grown from 1984 to 2004. If non-network television advertising revenue grew at the same rate, the proportion of revenue generated by network television commercials would have remained steady. Since the proportion of revenue generated by network television commercials decreased, we know that non-network television advertising revenue must have grown at a faster rate.

(E) We know nothing of what will happen in the future. Perhaps the proportion of revenue generated by non-network television commercials will climb, perhaps it will hold steady, or perhaps it will decline.

7. *Stem Cell Research*

Government restrictions have severely limited the amount of stem cell research American companies can conduct. Because of these restrictions, many American scientists who specialize in the field of stem cell research have signed long term contracts to work for foreign companies. Recently, Congress has proposed lifting all restrictions on stem cell research.

Which of the following statements can most properly be inferred from the information above?

(A) Some foreign companies that conduct stem cell research work under fewer restrictions than some American companies do.

(B) Because American scientists are under long-term contracts to foreign companies, there will be a significant influx of foreign professionals into the United States.

ManhattanGMAT Prep
the new standard

(C) In all parts of the world, stem cell research is dependent on the financial backing of local government.

(D) In the near future, American companies will no longer be at the forefront of stem cell research.

(E) If restrictions on stem cell research are lifted, many of the American scientists will break their contracts to return to American companies.

In this argument, a cause-and-effect relationship is presented between American scientists signing long-term contracts with foreign companies and the U.S. government's restrictions on stem cell research. This cause-and-effect relationship is the key to the correct answer.

(A) CORRECT. If American scientists signed contracts with foreign companies specifically *because of U.S. restrictions*, we can infer that the new companies they signed with operate under fewer restrictions. Therefore, at least some foreign companies must work under fewer restrictions than some American companies do.

(B) While it is possible that once the restrictions are banned American companies will want to hire more scientists and will seek them overseas, there are too many unknowns to draw this conclusion using the given premises.

(C) This passage is about government restrictions; we are given no information about financial backing.

(D) We are not given any information regarding America's current or future position in terms of stem cell research. Though government restrictions and scientists switching companies could be issues related to a company's prosperity, we are given no information about how these directly affect America's position.

(E) Though this might happen, we cannot conclude for certain that it will happen.

8. Gift Catalogue

Gift Catalogue Inc. sent seven custom-made gift packages last week. Last week, all of the shipments from Gift Catalogue Inc. that were sent out on Wednesday or later consisted entirely of non-custom-made gift packages. Gift Catalogue Inc. sent seven gift packages to Technocorp last week, at least two of which were custom-made gift packages.

If the statements in the passage above are true, which of the following must also be true about Gift Catalogue Inc.?

(A) At least one of the gift packages sent to Technocorp last week was not custom-made.

(B) At least one of the custom-made gift packages sent last week was not directed to Technocorp.

(C) The majority of the gift packages sent to Technocorp last week were sent on Wednesday or later.

(D) Some of the gift packages sent to Technocorp last week were sent on Tuesday or earlier.

(E) Technocorp received a higher proportion of the gift packages sent last week from Gift Catalogue Inc. than any other recipient.

This argument consists of a number of premises, and we are asked to find a conclusion that must follow from these premises. The first premise is that Gift Catalogue Inc. sent seven custom-made gift packages last week. The second premise is that all of the packages sent on Wednesday or later were not custom-made. The third premise is that seven gift packages were sent to Technocorp last week, and that at least two of these packages were custom-made.

(A) This may or may not be true. From the third premise, it may be the case that all seven gift packages sent to Technocorp last week were custom-made.

(B) This may or may not be true. From the first and third premises, it may be the case that all seven custom-made gift packages sent last week were sent to Technocorp.

(C) This may or may not be the case. From the third premise, it may be the case that all of the gift packages sent to Technocorp were custom-made and sent prior to Wednesday.

(D) CORRECT. In the third premise, it is stated that at least two of the gift packages sent to Technocorp were custom-made. In the second premise, it is stated that all gift packages sent on Wednesday or later were not custom-made. Therefore, it must be the case that some (at least two) of the gift packages sent to Technocorp last week were sent on Tuesday or earlier.

(E) This may or may not be the case. We have no information about the number of packages sent to companies other than Technocorp.

9. Mutual Funds

Many managers of mutual funds proclaim that they have been able to generate consistently higher rates of return on their investments than the general stock market by buying shares of undervalued companies. Classical economic theory, however, proposes the "efficient capital markets hypothesis," which indicates that stock prices accurately reflect the value of the underlying investments, incorporating all information available to the public. If the efficient capital markets hypothesis is correct, then it should be expected that _____.

(A) mutual fund managers, in order to compete with each other, will bid up the prices of certain stocks beyond their true values

(B) mutual fund managers use insider information, an illegal practice, to generate higher rates of return than the general stock market

(C) stock prices will rise over time

(D) given public information alone, companies cannot reliably be labeled undervalued or overvalued relative to the general stock market

(E) some mutual fund managers are better than others at generating a higher rate of return on investments

This argument first describes the claims of many mutual fund managers that they have been able to generate consistently higher rates of return than the general stock market. The argument also describes and defines the "efficient capital markets hypothesis" as the principle that stock prices

accurately reflecting all publicly available information. The question then asks for a conclusion that depends on the premise that the efficient capital markets hypothesis is correct.

(A) While the described event could occur, it would not be expected to occur as a consequence of the efficient capital markets hypothesis. The efficient capital markets hypothesis posits that stock prices accurately reflect the value of the underlying investments. Bidding up the price does not equate to an accurately-priced stock.

(B) Though it is possible that some mutual fund managers have engaged in insider trading, we do not have to conclude that mutual fund managers must do this as a consequence of the efficient capital markets theory in order to generate a high rate of return.

(C) The premises do not indicate that stock prices will rise over time. Stock prices will only rise according to the efficient capital markets hypothesis if the value of the underlying investments also rises over time.

(D) CORRECT. If the efficient capital markets hypothesis is correct, and stock prices accurately reflect the value of the underlying investments, incorporating public information, then if only public information is available, companies would not be either undervalued or overvalued; instead, they would be valued appropriately.

(E) While it is probably true in the real world that some mutual fund managers are more successful than others, it does not follow from the efficient capital markets hypothesis.

10. Real Estate Prices

In the last year, real estate prices, such as those for houses and condominiums, have gone up an average of 7% in the city of Galway but only 2% in the town of Tuam. On the other hand, average rents for apartments have risen 8% in Tuam over the last year, but only 4% in Galway.

Which of the following is an inference that can be reasonably drawn from the premises given above?

(A) In the last year, the ratio of average apartment rents to average real estate prices has increased in Tuam but fallen in Galway.
(B) Tuam has experienced a greater shift in demand toward the rental market than Galway has.
(C) It has become easier for Galway real estate to be bought and sold, whereas it has become easier for Tuam real estate to be rented.
(D) The supply of rental apartment units has decreased more in Tuam than in Galway.
(E) The average amount spent on housing is higher in Galway than it is in Tuam.

The question presents two trends in the real estate market in each of two cities and asks for an inference that can be drawn from these facts.

(A) CORRECT. In Tuam, rents have gone up at a faster rate (8%) than real estate prices (2%). Thus, the ratio of average rents to average real estate prices must have grown in that city—the numerator has grown faster than the denominator. In contrast, Galway rents have gone up at a slower rate (4%) than real estate prices (7%). Thus, the ratio of average rents to average real estate prices has actually decreased.

(B) It is not necessarily true that Tuam has experienced a greater shift in demand toward the rental market. For instance, the larger increase in Tuam rents could be explained by a reduction in the supply of rental units in Tuam.

(C) The premises do not indicate whether Galway real estate is easier or harder to be bought and sold, or whether Tuam real estate is easier or harder to be rented. The premises simply indicate the growth in prices and rents.

(D) It is not necessarily true that the supply of rental units has decreased more in Tuam than in Galway. For instance, there could be a sudden growth in demand in Tuam for rental units (e.g. because of an influx of young singles who are eager to rent), causing rents to increase more rapidly.

(E) The premises indicate nothing about the actual amounts of money spent in the two towns. We are given only percentage growth rates.

REAL GMAT PROBLEMS

Now that you have completed your study of DRAW A CONCLUSION questions, it is time to test your skills on passages that have actually appeared on real GMAT exams over the past several years.

The problem set below is composed of Critical Reasoning passages from two books published by GMAC (Graduate Management Admission Council):

The Official Guide for GMAT Review, 11th Edition (pages 32–38 & 468–504)
The Official Guide for GMAT Verbal Review (pages 116–142)

Diagram each argument. Then answer the question by drawing a conclusion supported by the premises in your diagram.

Note: Problem numbers preceded by "D" refer to questions in the Diagnostic Test chapter of *The Official Guide for GMAT Review, 11th Edition* (pages 32–38).

Draw a Conclusion
> *11th Edition:* 6, 19, 21, 31, 34, 35, 46, 51, 56, 57, 60, 66, 70, 71, 75, 76, 95, 101, 104, D24, D31
> *Verbal Review:* 2, 12, 14, 20, 43, 44, 52, 57, 59, 64, 74, 77

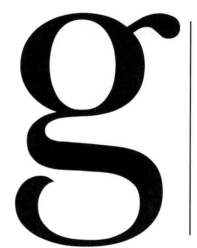

Chapter 6
of
CRITICAL REASONING

STRENGTHEN THE CONCLUSION

In This Chapter . . .

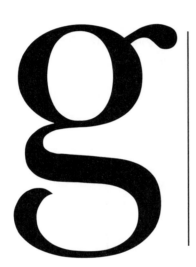

- Strengthen the Conclusion Overview
- Create an S-W-Slash Chart
- Decide Between Two Attractive Answer Choices
- Wrong Answer Choice Types

STRENGTHEN THE CONCLUSION

Strengthen the Conclusion questions ask you to provide additional support for a given conclusion. The question stem may appear in a number of forms:

> Which of the following, if true, most strengthens the argument above?

> Which of the following, if true, most strongly supports the scientists' hypothesis?

> Which of the following provides the strongest reason to expect that the plan will be successful?

A premise that strengthens the conclusion should do at least one of the following:

> (1) Fix a weakness of the conclusion, OR

> (2) Validate an assumption made by the argument, OR

> (3) Introduce additional supporting evidence.

Note that this is different from finding an assumption in that an assumption will generally be *necessary* for a conclusion to follow from the premises. A premise can *strengthen* or *support* a conclusion without being *necessary* for that conclusion.

The correct answer choice for a Strengthen question will typically function as a new premise. This choice will be related to the argument but generally introduce new information supporting the conclusion. A correct answer might provide an explanation of or support for a keyword in the conclusion. Alternatively, a correct answer might validate an assumption by providing a new piece of information that suggests that a particular assumption is indeed true.

Occasionally, a Strengthen the Conclusion question will ask you which answer choice does NOT strengthen the conclusion. For example:

> Each of the following, if true, would be helpful in arguing that the recycling program will achieve its goals EXCEPT:

The EXCEPT type of question also asks you to identify which answer choices serve to strengthen the conclusion, but in this case for the purpose of *eliminating* those answer choices. Note that the correct answer for this particular question need not actually weaken the conclusion—it just fails to strengthen the conclusion. As discussed in the "General Strategy" chapter of this guide, one way to handle EXCEPT questions is to simplify them by eliminating the word "EXCEPT" and replacing them with "NOT."

To strengthen an argument, look for an answer choice that fixes a weakness of the conclusion, validates an assumption, or introduces new supporting evidence.

Create an S-W-Slash Chart

The process of elimination in Strengthen the Conclusion questions takes on a very specific form. Write down A through E. Then, as you evaluate each answer choice, note down whether each answer

> 1. *strengthens* the conclusion (note with an "**S**"),
> 2. *weakens* the conclusion (note with a "**W**"),
> 3. or is *irrelevant* to the conclusion (note with a "**–**" or slash-through).

It is very easy to reverse your thinking and to get confused as you work with a difficult Strengthen problem. By keeping your assessments organized and on paper, you will save yourself time and effort, and you will be less likely to make a mistake.

At times it may not be entirely clear whether an answer choice strengthens or weakens the conclusion. For example, an answer choice may serve to strengthen the conclusion, but only in an indirect or arguable way. If that is the case, you might note the answer choice with a lowercase "**s**" in order to indicate that the answer choice may only marginally strengthen the conclusion. As you assess the other choices, determine whether you need to refine your categorization of that answer choice. Depending upon the other answer choices, it may be obvious that this answer choice is wrong or, alternatively, that it is the best answer.

In addition, the question may ask you to strengthen the *argument*, rather than the *conclusion* specifically. Do not be distracted: the test is using the word *argument* as a synonym for the conclusion. You still must specifically strengthen the conclusion.

Consider the following example:

> Compensation has not been the reason for the recent rash of employee departures at QuestCorp. Rather, the departures have been caused by employee dissatisfaction with poor working conditions and the absence of advancement opportunities.
>
> Which of the following, if true, would most support the claim made above as to the cause of departures from QuestCorp?
>
> (A) Many prospective hires at QuestCorp have expressed that their compensation is negotiable.
> (B) All employees at QuestCorp's main competitor recently received a large and well-publicized raise.
> (C) Many departing employees have cited abusive managers and unsafe factories as responsible for their decision to leave QuestCorp.
> (D) Studies indicate that compensation is one of several important factors regarding the decision to switch jobs.
> (E) QuestCorp has recently initiated a review of its internal policies, including those regarding working conditions and employee promotions.

The conclusion is that *the departures have been caused by employee dissatisfaction with poor working conditions and the absence of advancement opportunities.*

Sidebar:

Use an S-W-Slash chart to organize your answer choices right away. This way, you can avoid reading answer choices repeatedly.

Use an S-W-slash chart to categorize and eliminate answer choices.

Answer choice **(A)** is irrelevant to the conclusion. The argument discusses recently departed employees, not prospective hires.

Answer choice **(B)**, if anything, weakens the conclusion by suggesting that departing employees might have done so because they felt under-compensated.

Answer choice **(C)** strengthens the conclusion, providing examples of *poor working conditions* (*abusive managers and unsafe factories*) that were cited by departing employees. Notice that the choice does not need to make the conclusion definitively true; it just needs to make the conclusion more likely to be true. As always, we should continue to evaluate all answer choices.

Answer choice **(D)** is irrelevant. This answer choice refers to all employees, not the particular employees that quit QuestCorp.

Answer choice **(E)** could be considered to strengthen the conclusion; perhaps the rash of departures has led to the review. However, *internal policies* is very broad, and this answer choice requires us to assume a particular motivation for the review. In fact, it is unclear from the answer choice what has motivated the reexamination of policies; it may simply be an annually scheduled review. Answer choices that require additional assumptions or logical leaps to strengthen the conclusion will generally be incorrect. Answer choice **(E)** should be labeled either irrelevant, or perhaps a very indirect strengthen with a lowercase "**s**."

Answer choice **(C)** is correct.

As noted earlier, some questions will fall into the category of "EXCEPT" questions. Such a question might look something like this one:

Each of the following, if true, would be helpful in arguing that the recycling program will achieve its goals EXCEPT:

When you see an "EXCEPT" question, you must first classify it. Most of the time, it will be either a Strengthen the Conclusion or a Weaken the Conclusion (discussed in Chapter 7 of this guide). The question above is a Strengthen the Conclusion question. Then, realize that the wording says each answer choice *does* strengthen the conclusion EXCEPT for one. You should expect to find four choices that strengthen the conclusion and one choice that does not. The "odd choice out" may weaken the conclusion or it may simply be a irrelevant or neutral. As long as it does not strengthen, it is the right answer.

> Do not forget to identify and diagram the conclusion of the argument before you attempt to find an answer choice that strengthens it!

Decide Between Two Attractive Answer Choices

The S-W-Slash chart is an essential tool for eliminating incorrect answer choices. At worst, it usually helps you to narrow the possible answers down to two choices and prevents you from getting distracted by the wording of the question. Consider this example:

> Donut Chain, wishing to increase the profitability of its new store, will place a coupon in the local newspaper offering a free donut with a cup of coffee at its grand opening. Donut Chain calculates that the cost of the advertisement and the free donuts will be more than recouped by the new business generated through the promotion.
>
> Which of the following, if true, most strengthens the prediction that Donut Chain's promotion will increase the new store's profitability?
>
> (A) Donut Chain has a loyal following in much of the country.
> (B) Donut Chain has found that the vast majority of new visitors to its stores become regular customers.
> (C) Donuts at Donut Chain cost less than a cup of coffee.
> (D) Most of the copies of the coupon in the local newspaper will not be redeemed for free donuts.
> (E) Donut Chain's stores are generally very profitable.

The conclusion of this argument is that the promotion will increase the new store's profitability. We should look for an additional supporting premise, or a statement that somehow addresses a weakness of the argument, using our S-W-slash chart.

S A
S B
     ~~C~~
w D
     ~~E~~

Answer choice **(A)** could potentially be seen as supportive of the conclusion. Perhaps it indicates that Donut Chain's donuts are tasty and likely to promote repeat business. However, it is unstated whether the new store is in a part of the country in which Donut Chain enjoys a *loyal following,* nor do we even know whether the loyal following at other stores is enough to result in high or increasing profitability. Since the conclusion refers specifically to the profitability of the new store, answer choice **(A)** is irrelevant, or at best a very small "**s.**"

Answer choice **(B)** strengthens the argument. If the *vast majority* of Donut Chain's new visitors become regular customers, then a substantial proportion of those who redeem the coupon can be expected to make repeat visits. This is one essential component of profitability, as this information makes clear that the promotion will generate revenue for the long-term.

Answer choice **(C)** is irrelevant. The fact that a cup of coffee is more expensive than a donut does not determine long-term or overall profitability. Also, this choice does not take into account the cost of the advertisement.

Answer choice **(D)** weakens the argument. If most of the copies of the coupon are not redeemed, the promotion is unlikely to generate substantial new business, thereby limiting the promotion's ability to generate increased revenue and profit.

*Manhattan*GMAT*Prep*
the new standard

Answer choice **(E)** is irrelevant. The fact that Donut Chain's other stores are profitable in general is not germane to whether this particular promotion will <u>increase</u> the new store's profitability.

Now, a review of the two answer choices indicates that there are still two possibilities, **(A)** and **(B)**. Because answer choice **(A)** requires additional assumptions to strengthen the conclusion significantly, answer choice **(B)** is correct.

Wrong Answer Choice Types

The common categories of wrong answers for Strengthen the Conclusion questions are essentially the same as those for Find the Assumption questions.

A. No Tie to the Conclusion

Many wrong answers will be tied to a premise but not to the conclusion. The answer choice could simply provide unnecessary information about that premise. For instance, consider answer choice **(C)** to the Donut Chain problem above:

> (C) Donuts at Donut Chain cost less than a cup of coffee.

This answer choice may relate to the revenue lost by giving away free donuts, but it does not clearly impact the conclusion.

Alternatively, a "No Tie to the Conclusion" answer choice could <u>support</u> that premise, but if the premise is already stated as a fact, it does not need support. A wrong answer of this type for the Donut Chain argument might read as follows: *Donut Chain expects that the cost of advertising the promotion will total only 60% of the expected profits from the new business that the promotion will generate.* This provides evidence for the second premise, but we already know that the second premise is true.

A few wrong answers with "No Tie to the Conclusion" do bring in language from the conclusion, but they do not meaningfully support the conclusion. Deceptive answers such as these <u>seem</u> relevant. Make sure that the answer you choose is not simply related to the conclusion, but in fact supports it. Consider this deceptive answer for the Donut Chain argument: *New Donut Chain stores generally become more profitable over time.* This seems related to the conclusion, which contains the words *increase the new store's profitability.* However, the wrong answer does not address whether the <u>promotion</u> will cause this increase.

Also, recall that some wrong answers can be "Real-World Plausible." You are not assessing a choice's truth in the real world—only whether the choice strengthens the argument.

B. Wrong Direction

Many wrong answers on Strengthen questions in fact weaken the argument. Make sure that you note whether a particular question is a Strengthen the Conclusion or a Weaken the Conclusion question so that you do not mistakenly pick the wrong answer. In the Donut Chain problem, answer choice **(D)** is an example of this deceptive answer type:

> (D) Most of the copies of the coupon in the local newspaper will not be redeemed for free donuts.

Problem Set

Use the skills you have just learned to answer the following Strengthen the Conclusion questions and create an S-W-Slash chart for each set of answer choices. Be sure to diagram each argument. Detailed answers and explanations follow this problem set.

1. Sneakers

Brand X designs and builds custom sneakers, one sneaker at a time. It recently announced plans to sell "The Gold Standard," a sneaker that will cost five times more to manufacture than any other sneaker that has been ever been created.

Which of the following, if true, most supports the prediction that The Gold Standard shoe line will be profitable?

(A) Because of its reputation as an original and exclusive sneaker, The Gold Standard will be favored by urban hipsters willing to pay exceptionally high prices in order to stand out.
(B) Of the last four new sneakers that Brand X has released, three have sold at a rate that was higher than projected.
(C) A rival brand recently declared bankruptcy and ceased manufacturing shoes.
(D) The market for The Gold Standard will not be more limited than the market for other Brand X shoes.
(E) The Gold Standard is made using canvas that is more than five times the cost of the canvas used in most sneakers.

2. Farmsley Center

The Farmsley Center for the Performing Arts, designed by a world-renowned architect, was built ten years ago in downtown Metropolis. A recent study shows that, on average, a person who attends a performance at the Farmsley Center spends eighty-three dollars at downtown businesses on the day of the performance. Citing this report, the chairman of the Farmsley Center's Board of Trustees contends that the Farmsley Center has been a significant source of the economic revitalization of downtown Metropolis.

Which of the following, if true, most strongly supports the chairman's contention?

(A) The Metropolis Chamber of Commerce honored the Farmsley chairman this year for his contributions to the city.
(B) Restaurants near the Farmsley Center tend to be more expensive than restaurants in outlying areas.
(C) The Farmsley Center is the only building in Metropolis designed by a world-renowned contemporary architect.
(D) For major theater companies on national tours, the Farmsley Center is the first choice among venues in downtown Metropolis.
(E) Many suburbanites visit downtown Metropolis on weekends primarily in order to see performances at the Farmsley Center.

3. Airline Connection

John was flying from San Francisco to New York with a connecting flight in Chicago on the same airline. Chicago's airport is one of the largest in the world, consisting of several small stand-alone terminals connected by trams. John's plane arrived on time. John was positive he would make his connecting flight thirty minutes later, because _____.

Which of the following most logically completes the argument above?

(A) John's airline is known for always being on time
(B) a number of other passengers on John's first flight were also scheduled to take John's connecting flight.
(C) at the airport in Chicago, airlines always fly into and out of the same terminal
(D) John knew there was another flight to New York scheduled for one hour after the connecting flight he was scheduled to take
(E) the airline generally closes the doors of a particular flight ten minutes before it is scheduled to take off

4. Digital Video Recorders

Advertising Executive: More than 10 million American households now own digital video recorders which can fast-forward over television commercials; approximately 75% of these households fast-forward over at least one commercial per 30-minute program. Television commercials are now much less cost-effective, as they are not as widely watched as they used to be.

Which of the following, if true, strengthens the claim that television commercials are less cost-effective than they used to be?

(A) Product placement within television programs is a viable alternative to traditional television commercials.
(B) The television programs preferred by consumers without digital video recorders are similar to those preferred by consumers with the devices.
(C) Prior to the advent of digital video recorders, very few television viewers switched channels or left the room when commercials began
(D) The cost-effectiveness of television advertising is based less upon how many people watch a particular commercial and more upon the appropriateness of the demographic.
(E) Due to an imperfect sampling system used to measure the number of viewers, many companies find it difficult to determine the return on investment for television commercials.

5. Sunrise Splash

Company Management: The most recent advertising campaign for our leading brand of low-calorie soft drinks, Sunrise Splash, has obviously been a success. Since this campaign was conducted in several magazines a year ago, our unit sales of Sunrise Splash have increased by 10%, reaching a record level in our corporate history. In addition, consumer surveys indicate that the proportion of customers who recognize this brand has nearly doubled over this period.

Which of the following statements would most strongly support the claim made about the campaign's success?

(A) Over the past year, the price of Sunrise Splash has been reduced by nearly 20%.

(B) Over the past year, unit sales of Sunrise Splash have increased by nearly 1.5 million bottles.

(C) As a result of a shift in consumer preferences towards low-calorie soft drinks, the consumption of these drinks has grown at a double-digit rate over the past several years.

(D) The majority of new sales of Sunrise Splash made over the past year involved one of the coupons distributed during the last advertising campaign.

(E) Over the past year, the company has experienced a dramatic increase in sales of many other soft drinks.

6. XYZ Profits

The CEO of Corporation XYZ was very excited about the company's 2006 fourth quarter performance. Sales of the company's newest product were double the fourth quarter target projections while product costs remained consistent with estimates. The CEO projected that due to these increased sales, the company's profits for the fourth quarter would dramatically exceed the company's prior expectations.

Which of the following, if true, supports the CEO's projection?

(A) Most of the products sold by Corporation XYZ are manufactured goods that tend to be replaced by consumers every couple of years.

(B) In the fourth quarter, Corporation XYZ's older, less up-to-date products were often sold at a substantial discount by retailers.

(C) The profit margins of Corporation XYZ's newest product are higher than the industry average.

(D) Reviews of Corporation XYZ's newest product in magazines and blogs have been uniformly positive.

(E) The newest product represents the vast majority of Corporation XYZ's projected revenue for the fourth quarter of 2006.

7. E-mailed Coupons

The redemption rate for e-mailed coupons is far lower than that for traditionally distributed paper coupons. One factor is the "digital divide"—those who might benefit the most from using coupons, such as homemakers, the elderly and those in low-income households, often do not have the knowledge or equipment necessary to go online and receive coupons.

Which of the following, if true, does the most to support the claim that the digital divide is responsible for lower electronic coupon redemption rates?

(A) Computers are available for free in libraries, schools, and community centers.

(B) The redemption rate of ordinary coupons is particularly high among elderly and low income people that do not know how to use computers.

(C) Many homes, including those of elderly and low income people, do not have high speed Internet connections.

(D) More homemakers than elderly people would use computers if they had access to them.

(E) The redemption rate for coupons found on the Internet has risen in the last five years.

8. NASA

If life exists elsewhere in the solar system, scientists suspect it would most likely be on Europa, an ice covered moon orbiting Jupiter. However, NASA recently scrapped an unmanned science mission to Europa and reassigned most of the employees involved in the project to another project which focuses on landing an astronaut on Mars. Polls show that Americans are far more fascinated by space travel than they are by discovering life elsewhere in the universe. Critics argue that NASA's decision-making process places a greater emphasis on public interest than it does on the importance of scientific research.

Which of the following, if true, would most strengthen NASA's contention that the critics are misinformed?

(A) In 2007, NASA will spend 30% of its total budget on developing a space shuttle that can travel to Mars. In 2013, that figure is expected to drop to 0%.

(B) Studies have shown that Congress traditionally determines NASA's budget by assessing public interest in NASA's projects.

(C) Some scientists are convinced that a mission to Europa would add immeasurably to our understanding of the universe; others believe that we will gain little insight from exploring Europa.

(D) A new telescope that has been developed in Tokyo allows scientists to look at Europa in ways never possible before and promises to yield more information than the planned mission was designed to provide.

(E) Most Americans feel that a shuttle to Mars is the next logical step in the development of a system that will eventually allow humans to travel to places as far away as Europa and beyond.

9. Deep-Brain Stimulation

Scientist: An experimental technique for combating severe depression, deep-brain stimulation (DBS) demonstrates much promise for the long-term treatment of chronic depression. In a recent experiment, electrodes were implanted into the brains of six patients who had not responded to any currently approved treatment for depression. When an electrical current to the electrodes was switched on, four of the patients reported feeling a dramatic reduction of depressive symptoms. The depressive symptoms returned when the current was switched off.

Which of the following, if true, best supports the scientist's claim of the promising potential usage of DBS?

(A) The electrodes implanted during deep-brain stimulation can only be activated in a hospital setting.

(B) The other two patients reported a slight reduction of depressive symptoms when the current to their electrodes was activated.

(C) The operation to implant the electrodes poses a serious risk of brain hemorrhage, infection or seizure.

(D) Continuous stimulation of the electrodes produced sustained remission from depression in the four patients for six months.

(E) Deep-brain stimulation relies on the expertise of highly skilled physicians.

10. Inca Trail

In 2001 the Peruvian government began requiring tourists to buy expensive permits to hike the remote Inca Trail, which goes to the ancient city of Machu Picchu. The total number of permits is strictly limited; in fact, only 500 people per day are now allowed to hike the Inca Trail, whereas before 2001 daily visitors numbered in the thousands. The Peruvian government claims that this permit program has successfully prevented deterioration of archaeological treasures along the Inca Trail.

Which of the following, if true, most strengthens the argument above?

(A) Since 2001, tourist guides along the Inca Trail have received 50% to 100% increases in take-home pay.

(B) Villages near Machu Picchu have experienced declines in income, as fewer tourists buy fewer craft goods and refreshments.

(C) Many of the funds from the sale of Inca Trail permits are used to staff a museum of Incan culture in Lima, Peru's capital, and to hire guards for archaeological sites without permit programs.

(D) Since 2001, Incan ruins similar to Machu Picchu but not on the Inca Trail have disintegrated at a significantly greater rate than those on the Inca Trail.

(E) The total number of tourists in Peru has risen substantially since 2001, even as the number of tourists hiking the Inca Trail has remained constant.

1. Sneakers

Brand X designs and builds custom sneakers, one sneaker at a time. It recently announced plans to sell "The Gold Standard," a sneaker that will cost five times more to manufacture than any other sneaker that has been ever been created.

Which of the following, if true, most supports the prediction that The Gold Standard shoe line will be profitable?

(A) Because of its reputation as an original and exclusive sneaker, The Gold Standard will be favored by urban hipsters willing to pay exceptionally high prices in order to stand out.

(B) Of the last four new sneakers that Brand X has released, three have sold at a rate that was higher than projected.

(C) A rival brand recently declared bankruptcy and ceased manufacturing shoes.

(D) The market for The Gold Standard will not be more limited than the market for other Brand X shoes.

(E) The Gold Standard is made using canvas that is more than five times the cost of the canvas used in most sneakers.

The conclusion is located in the question: the prediction that The Gold Standard shoe line will be profitable. In the passage, we have been given information that seems to run counter to this conclusion—the costs of manufacturing this shoe are exceptionally high. We can think of profit as revenue minus cost. If costs are exceptionally high, the only way a profit can be made is if revenue is also exceptionally high.

(A) CORRECT. Strengthen. If urban hipsters are willing to pay exceptionally high prices, the exceptionally high costs might be offset enough for the shoe line to be profitable.

(B) Irrelevant. A higher sales rate than projected does not actually give us any information about profitability. In any case, the results of past releases are not necessarily indicative of the case at hand.

(C) Irrelevant. One can argue that this is good for Brand X, in that it will mean that there is one less competitor, or that this is bad for Brand X, in that it is indicative of a sagging sneaker market. In any case, there is no direct connection between this rival brand and the potential profitability of The Gold Standard.

(D) Irrelevant. We have been told nothing that connects the market to profitability. We also lack information about the profitability of past sneakers.

(E) Irrelevant. This is perhaps one reason why manufacturing costs are so high, but we already knew the costs were high from the argument. This choice does not in any way support the conclusion that the new sneaker will be profitable.

2. Farmsley Center

The Farmsley Center for the Performing Arts, designed by a world-renowned architect, was built ten years ago in downtown Metropolis. A recent study shows that, on average, a person who attends a performance at the Farmsley Center spends eighty-three dollars at downtown businesses on the day of the performance. Citing this report, the

chairman of the Farmsley Center's Board of Trustees contends that the Farmsley Center has been a significant source of the economic revitalization of downtown Metropolis.

Which of the following, if true, most strongly supports the chairman's contention?

(A) The Metropolis Chamber of Commerce honored the Farmsley chairman this year for his contributions to the city.
(B) Restaurants near the Farmsley Center tend to be more expensive than restaurants in outlying areas.
(C) The Farmsley Center is the only building in Metropolis designed by a world-renowned contemporary architect.
(D) For major theater companies on national tours, the Farmsley Center is the first choice among venues in downtown Metropolis.
(E) Many suburbanites visit downtown Metropolis on weekends primarily in order to see performances at the Farmsley Center.

The chairman claims that same-day spending at downtown businesses by people attending performances at the Farmsley Center has contributed to the economic revitalization of downtown Metropolis. His argument depends on it being true that this spending represents an increased flow of money into the economy of downtown Metropolis. If, for example, the $83 per visitor that he cites is money that would have been spent in downtown businesses even if the Farmsley Center had not been built, the chairman's argument would be unsound.

(A) Irrelevant. We do not know what contributions to the city the business group has in mind. Perhaps the chairman is being honored for founding and running a non-profit soup kitchen. The choice does not support the specific conclusion that the Farmsley center has helped with Metropolis' economic revitalization.

(B) Irrelevant. Expensive restaurants may be a sign of the economic revitalization of downtown Metropolis, but they do not tell us what causal factors led to that revitalization.

(C) Irrelevant. In the absence of information specifically relating the architecture of the Farmsley Center to spending at downtown businesses, we cannot say that the architect's international standing has helped in the economic revitalization downtown.

(D) Irrelevant. The Farmsley Center may be hosting performances that would otherwise have taken place at other downtown venues, but this does not mean that extra money is being spent downtown.

(E) **CORRECT.** Strengthen. If suburbanites are coming to Metropolis primarily in order to see performances at the Farmsley Center, and each person also spends $83, on average, at other businesses, this choice supports the idea that the Farmsley Center has contributed to the economic revitalization of downtown Metropolis. Notice, by the way, that this information by no means constitutes iron-clad proof of the chairman's contention. Since this is a Strengthen the Conclusion question, however, you do not need to find an answer choice that proves the conclusion—just one that makes the conclusion more likely.

3. Airline Connection

John was flying from San Francisco to New York with a connecting flight in Chicago on the same airline. Chicago's airport is one of the largest in the world, consisting of several small stand-alone terminals connected by trams. John's plane arrived on time. John was positive he would make his connecting flight thirty minutes later, because _____.

Which of the following most logically completes the argument above?

(A) John's airline is known for always being on time
(B) a number of other passengers on John's first flight were also scheduled to take John's connecting flight
(C) at the airport in Chicago, airlines always fly in and out of the same terminal
(D) John knew there was another flight to New York scheduled for one hour after the connecting flight he was scheduled to take
(E) the airline generally closes the doors of a particular flight ten minutes before it is scheduled to take off

This argument addresses John's concern about making a connecting flight. The airport with the connecting flight is very large, consisting of several small stand-alone terminals. The correct answer choice will support John in concluding that he can likely make his connecting flight thirty minutes later despite the size of the airport.

(A) Irrelevant. This is a general observation about the timeliness of John's airline, but it does not provide any new information—it is already established in the premises that John's particular flight arrived on time. The fact that his connecting flight will likely depart on time may even weaken the argument.

(B) Irrelevant. Airlines have been known to delay flights in order to ensure that a large number of passengers can make the connection, but we should not have to make an additional assumption in order to be able to say that this choice strengthens the given conclusion.

(C) CORRECT. Strengthen. This answer choice provides information that John will not have to leave his terminal in order to reach his connecting flight. The premises describe the terminals as "small." This information provides us with the strongest piece of information that suggests John will be able to make his flight within thirty minutes.

(D) Irrelevant. The following flight has no bearing on John's ability to catch the flight on which he is currently booked.

(E) Irrelevant/weaken. If anything, this choice weakens the idea that John will catch the connecting flight by shortening the length of time he has to get to the second flight's gate.

4. Digital Video Recorders

Advertising Executive: More than 10 million American households now own digital video recorders which can fast-forward over television commercials; approximately 75% of these households fast-forward over at least one commercial per 30-minute program. Television commercials are now much less cost-effective as they are not as widely watched as they used to be.

Which of the following, if true, strengthens the claim that television commercials are less cost-effective than they used to be?

(A) Product placement within television programs is a viable alternative to tradition-al television commercials.

(B) The television programs preferred by consumers without digital video recorders are similar to those preferred by consumers with the devices.

(C) Prior to the advent of digital video recorders, very few television viewers switched channels or left the room when commercials began.

(D) The cost-effectiveness of television advertising is based less upon how many peo-ple watch a particular commercial and more upon the appropriateness of the demographic.

(E) Due to an imperfect sampling system used to measure the number of viewers, many companies find it difficult to determine the return on investment for tele-vision commercials.

The advertising executive presents the following facts: millions of households can fast-forward over commercials and a large percentage fast-forward over at least one commercial per 30-minute pro-gram. The executive concludes in the final sentence that the cost-effectiveness of television commer-cials is dropping as television commercials are not as widely watched as they used to be.

(A) Irrelevant. This does not address the given sequence of events and cannot therefore support the conclusion about traditional television commercials.

(B) Irrelevant. Any similarity or difference in preference of television programs for different con-sumers is beyond the scope of this argument, which addresses the effectiveness of advertising.

(C) CORRECT. Strengthen. The argument makes a claim that television commercials are not as widely watched as they used to be but only provides information about today's commercial viewing habits, not those in the past. This choice provides the remaining information to show that commercials very likely are not watched as frequently as they used to be.

(D) Weaken. Though this may be true in general, it does not support the ad executive's conclusion; in fact, it undermines it. If the number of people watching the commercial does not matter as much as something else, then the executive should not base his conclusion on this information.

(E) Irrelevant. Although this may be true in general, it does not support the given conclusion. Any difficulty in measuring return on investment does not strengthen or weaken the claim that tele-vision commercials have become increasingly less cost-effective.

5. Sunrise Splash

> Company Management: The most recent advertising campaign for our leading brand of low-calorie soft drinks, Sunrise Splash, has obviously been a success. Since this campaign was conducted in several magazines a year ago, our unit sales of Sunrise Splash have increased by 10%, reaching a record level in our company's history. In addition, consumer surveys indicate that the proportion of customers who recognize this brand has nearly doubled over this period.
>
> Which of the following statements would most strongly support the claim made about the campaign's success?
>
> (A) Over the past year, the price of Sunrise Splash has been reduced by nearly 20%.
> (B) Over the past year, unit sales of Sunrise Splash have increased by nearly 1.5 million bottles.
> (C) As a result of a shift in consumer preferences towards low-calorie soft drinks, the consumption of these drinks has grown at a double-digit rate over the past several years.
> (D) The majority of new sales of Sunrise Splash made over the past year involved one of the coupons distributed during the last advertising campaign.
> (E) Over the past year, the company has experienced a dramatic increase in sales of many other soft drinks.

In this argument, the company management concludes that the advertising campaign for Sunrise Splash was a success, citing the evidence of an increase in sales and brand recognition that followed this campaign. To support this argument, we need to demonstrate that the increase in sales and brand recognition indeed resulted from the campaign rather than from other market factors.

(A) Weaken. This answer choice introduces an alternative explanation that challenges the management claim. The increase in unit sales of the drink could have been caused by the reduction in prices rather than by the effectiveness of the advertising campaign.

(B) Irrelevant. This answer choice provides the actual increase in the number of units of Sunrise Splash sold over the past year but fails to establish the relationship between this increase and the effectiveness of the advertising campaign.

(C) Weaken. This answer demonstrates that the increase in sales of Sunrise Splash is likely to have been caused by the market trends favoring low-calorie consumer soft drinks in general. Note that without further information, we cannot assume that the shift in consumer preferences was a direct result of the advertising campaign.

(D) CORRECT. Strengthen. This answer choice strengthens the argument by demonstrating that the increase in sales was likely caused by the advertising campaign, since the majority of new purchases involved coupons distributed as part of that campaign.

(E) Irrelevant. Since the argument is focused on Sunrise Splash, evidence about other soft drinks produced by the company is out of scope.

6. XYZ Profits

The CEO of Corporation XYZ was very excited about the company's 2006 fourth quarter performance. Sales of the company's newest product were double the fourth quarter target projections while product costs remained consistent with estimates. The CEO projected that due to these increased sales, the company's profits for the fourth quarter would dramatically exceed the company's prior expectations.

Which of the following, if true, supports the CEO's projection?

(A) Most of the products sold by Corporation XYZ are manufactured goods that tend to be replaced by consumers every couple of years.

(B) In the fourth quarter, Corporation XYZ's older, less up-to-date products were often sold at a substantial discount by retailers.

(C) The profit margins of Corporation XYZ's newest product are higher than the industry average.

(D) Reviews of Corporation XYZ's newest product in magazines and blogs have been uniformly positive.

(E) The newest product represents the vast majority of Corporation XYZ's project- ed revenue for the fourth quarter of 2006.

The argument concerns Corporation XYZ's 2006 fourth quarter profits. It presents evidence that its most recent product has doubled sales projections, while keeping costs in line with initial projec- tions. The company's CEO then projected that the company's overall profits would dramatically exceed previously expected profit levels in the fourth quarter. If we study the evidence provided, it is unclear whether the sales of the new product comprise a high enough proportion of Corporation XYZ's revenues to result in the company *dramatically* exceeding profitability projections. The cor- rect answer choice will help to address this gap.

(A) Irrelevant. The periodic replacement of products manufactured by Corporation XYZ does not affect whether Corporation XYZ's profits would be dramatically higher than originally expected in the fourth quarter of 2006.

(B) Weaken. The fact that older products manufactured by Corporation XYZ are sold at a substan- tial discount weakens the CEO's conclusion in two ways. First, it suggests lower profits in the fourth quarter. Second, it indicates that Corporation XYZ's new product was just one of several products manufactured by the Company, suggesting that the success of the one product may not indicate high profits overall.

(C) Irrelevant. The fact that the new product enjoys higher profit margins than the industry average does not indicate that Corporation XYZ as a whole enjoyed dramatically higher profits than initially expected in the fourth quarter. It is also unknown how high industry profit margins are—they could be very small on average.

(D) Irrelevant. This answer choice is tempting in that it indicates why the new product may be sell- ing well. However, it is already established in the premises that sales of the new product are exceeding projections. The fact that the new product is well-reviewed does not affect whether Corporation XYZ as a whole dramatically exceeded its profitability projections for the fourth quarter.

*Manhattan*GMAT*Prep
the new standard

(E) CORRECT. Strengthen. If the vast majority of the projected revenue in the fourth quarter of 2006 was to come from the new product, the additional success of the new product would indicate that the Company as a whole would be likely to exceed projected profit for the quarter. This answer choice effectively eliminates the biggest concern with the CEO's projection—that the new product represents a small proportion of Corporation XYZ's revenues.

7. E-mailed Coupons

The redemption rate for e-mailed coupons is far lower than that for traditionally distributed paper coupons. One factor is the "digital divide"—those who might benefit the most from using coupons, such as homemakers, the elderly and those in low-income households, often do not have the knowledge or equipment necessary to go online and receive coupons.

Which of the following, if true, does the most to support the claim that the digital divide is responsible for lower electronic coupon redemption rates?

(A) Computers are available for free in libraries, schools, and community centers.
(B) The redemption rate of ordinary coupons is particularly high among elderly and low income people that do not know how to use computers.
(C) Many homes, including those of elderly and low income people, do not have high speed Internet connections.
(D) More homemakers than elderly people would use computers if they had access to them.
(E) The redemption rate for coupons found on the Internet has risen in the last five years.

The argument concludes that the *"digital divide"* is a reason for low redemption rates for e-mailed coupons because many people who would be likely to use such coupons lack computer access or familiarity. To strengthen this argument, one should either remove alternate possibilities or reinforce the given relationship.

(A) Weaken. This choice provides evidence that most people have access to computers, which would weaken the impact of any *"digital divide."*

(B) CORRECT. Strengthen. This choice provides further evidence for the conclusion by stipulating that ordinary coupons are redeemed at high levels by the elderly and low-income individuals. If this group does not have access to e-mailed coupons, this would explain in part the lower redemption rate of e-mailed coupons.

(C) Irrelevant. The fact that many homes lack high-speed Internet connections is irrelevant to the conclusion. There is no evidence that high-speed connections are necessary to utilize e-mailed coupons.

(D) Irrelevant. The argument treats homemakers and elderly people as part of a homogeneous group; making a distinction between them does not affect the conclusion.

(E) Irrelevant. The argument concerns conditions today and specifically compares two different forms of coupons (electronic and printed). The trend in redemption of electronic coupons does not affect the conclusion.

8. NASA

If life exists elsewhere in the solar system, scientists suspect it would most likely be on Europa, an ice covered moon orbiting Jupiter. However, NASA recently scrapped an unmanned science mission to Europa and reassigned most of the employees involved in the project to another project which focuses on landing an astronaut on Mars. Polls show that Americans are far more fascinated by space travel than they are by discovering life elsewhere in the universe. Critics argue that NASA's decision-making process places a greater emphasis on public interest than it does on the importance of scientific research.

Which of the following, if true, would most strengthen NASA's contention that its critics are misinformed?

(A) In 2007, NASA will spend 30% of its total budget on developing a space shuttle that can travel to Mars; in 2013, that figure is expected to drop to 0%.

(B) Studies have shown that Congress traditionally determines NASA's budget by assessing public interest in NASA's projects.

(C) Some scientists are convinced that a mission to Europa would add immeasurably to our understanding of the universe; others believe that we will gain little insight from exploring Europa.

(D) A new telescope that has been developed in Tokyo allows scientists to look at Europa in ways never possible before and promises to yield more information than the planned mission was designed to provide.

(E) Most Americans feel that a shuttle to Mars is the next logical step in the development of a system that will eventually allow humans to travel to places as far away as Europa and beyond.

The question tells us that NASA argues that its critics are misinformed. The critics believe that the decision to scrap the Europa project and those employees to the Mars project demonstrates that NASA is more interested in public opinion that scientific research. While it is true that most of the Europa employees were reassigned to the mission to Mars, no information was given about why the Europa project was scrapped in the first place.

(A) Irrelevant. The conclusion is based on the critics' opinions on causation, and this answer fails to address the issue of what motivated NASA in its decision-making process. Beware of reading too deeply into the information presented. The fact that the percentage of spending is going to go down could indicate many possible scenarios. Perhaps NASA is unhappy with the progress of the project and plans to cut future spending or maybe NASA expects the development of the shuttle to be completed by 2013.

(B) Weaken. If public interest determines its budget, NASA has strong motivation to keep public interest high. Additionally, this choice concerns NASA's *budget*, which is not a factor in the original argument.

(C) Irrelevant. This statement differentiates between the opinions of some scientists and the opinions of others, but sheds no light on the motivations behind NASA's decisions. Not only is the answer choice only indirectly related to our conclusion, it also adds very little new information.

*Manhattan*GMAT*Prep
the new standard

(D)CORRECT. Strengthen. This answer choice provides an alternate reason why NASA scrapped its plan for sending an unmanned vessel to Europa—the Tokyo telescope provides the information NASA would have attained from the mission, making the mission unnecessary.

(E) Irrelevant. The conclusion deals with NASA's motivations; this statement is about the inclinations of American citizens. There is no direct relationship between what Americans see as the future of space exploration and the motivations behind NASA's decision-making.

9. Deep-Brain Stimulation

Scientist: An experimental technique for combating severe depression, deep-brain stimulation (DBS) demonstrates much promise for the long-term treatment of chronic depression. In a recent experiment, electrodes were implanted into the brains of six patients who had not responded to any currently approved treatment for depression. When an electrical current to the electrodes was switched on, four of the patients reported feeling a dramatic reduction of depressive symptoms. The depressive symptoms returned when the current was switched off.

Which of the following, if true, best supports the scientist's claim of the promising potential usage of DBS?

(A) The electrodes implanted during deep-brain stimulation can only be activated in a hospital setting.
(B) The other two patients reported a slight reduction of depressive symptoms when the current to their electrodes was activated.
(C) The operation to implant the electrodes poses a serious risk of brain hemorrhage, infection or seizure.
(D) In a subsequent experiment, a one-hour treatment the electrodes produced sustained remission from depression in the four patients for six months.
(E) Deep-brain stimulation relies on the expertise of highly skilled physicians.

The argument claims that deep-brain stimulation is a promising long-term treatment for depression and further explains that, in a recent test, four of six patients reported an immediate and dramatic, but temporary, reduction of their depressive symptoms. The question asks us to support the scientist's claim that deep-brain stimulation is a promising *long-term* treatment for chronic depression. Thus, the correct answer must address the long-term effects of the treatment as the evidence presented only discusses short-term relief.

(A) Weaken. If the electrodes can only be activated in a hospital setting, deep-brain stimulation would be impractical as a long-term treatment since patients would have to remain in the hospital to receive the benefits of the treatment.

(B) Irrelevant. The fact that the other two patients received a minor immediate benefit from deep-brain stimulation in no way supports the long-term use of the procedure.

(C) Irrelevant/weaken. If anything, the severe risks associated with deep-brain stimulation undermine its potential as a long-term treatment for chronic depression.

(D) CORRECT. Strengthen. According to this answer choice, the immediate benefits perceived by the four patients were maintained over a period of six months. Thus, deep-brain stimulation seems to demonstrate long-term effectiveness.

(E) Irrelevant. The level of expertise needed to perform the procedure is not relevant to the long-term effectiveness of the procedure.

10. Inca Trail

In 2001 the Peruvian government began requiring tourists to buy expensive permits to hike the remote Inca Trail, which goes to the ancient city of Machu Picchu. The total number of permits is strictly limited; in fact, only 500 people per day are now allowed to hike the Inca Trail, whereas before 2001 daily visitors numbered in the thousands. The Peruvian government claims that this permit program has successfully prevented deterioration of archaeological treasures along the Inca Trail.

Which of the following, if true, most strengthens the argument above?

(A) Since 2001, tourist guides along the Inca Trail have received 50% to 100% increases in take-home pay.
(B) Villages near Machu Picchu have experienced declines in income, as fewer tourists buy fewer craft goods and refreshments.
(C) Many of the funds from the sale of Inca Trail permits are used to staff a museum of Incan culture in Lima, Peru's capital, and to hire guards for archaeological sites without permit programs.
(D) Since 2001, Incan ruins similar to Machu Picchu but not on the Inca Trail have disintegrated at a significantly greater rate than those on the Inca Trail.
(E) The total number of tourists in Peru has risen substantially since 2001, even as the number of tourists hiking the Inca Trail has remained constant.

According to the text, the Peruvian government claims that Inca Trail treasures would have deteriorated without a new permit program that has restricted the number of tourists. Supporting statements would likely emphasize one of the following two ideas:

One: A high number of tourists causes the deterioration of Inca Trail archaeological sites, and so a reduced number reduces the deterioration. Note that this causal connection, while reasonable, *cannot* be assumed.

Two: Other results of the permit program (e.g. new revenue) help prevent archaeological damage along the Inca Trail.

(A) Irrelevant. The increase in pay may have resulted from the permit program, and it may be reasonable to assume that this increase in pay has led to greater satisfaction in the job and hence, perhaps, to greater care for historical artifacts. However, this chain of reasoning is too speculative to strengthen the argument appreciably.

(B) Irrelevant. Local villages may have seen a drop in income as a result of the restrictions on tourist numbers, but this does not strengthen or weaken the claim that the permit program prevented Inca Trail ruins from deteriorating.

the new standard

(C) Irrelevant. The funds are a positive result of the permit program, but if these funds are used to protect or preserve archaeology elsewhere, then they do not impact the preservation of ruins specifically on the Inca Trail.

(D) CORRECT. Strengthen. The more rapid deterioration of similar ruins elsewhere supports the claim that that the permit program has helped prevent deterioration of Inca Trail ruins. Notice that this evidence does not rise to the level of absolute proof; other differences between the ruins might explain the different rates of deterioration. This choice does make it more likely, however, that the permit program has been successful in preserving the Inca Trail ruins, and that is sufficient for a Strengthen The Conclusion question.

(E) Irrelevant. Without the permit program, it is possible (though far from certain) that the number of tourists hiking the Inca Trail would have risen together with the total number of tourists in Peru. However, an increase in the number of tourists on the Inca Trail would not necessarily have led to greater deterioration of archaeological treasures on the trail.

REAL GMAT PROBLEMS

Now that you have completed your study of STRENGTHEN THE CONCLUSION questions, it is time to test your skills on passages that have actually appeared on real GMAT exams over the past several years.

The problem set below is composed of Critical Reasoning passages from two books published by GMAC (Graduate Management Admission Council):

The Official Guide for GMAT Review, 11th Edition (pages 32–38 & 468–504)
The Official Guide for GMAT Verbal Review (pages 116–142)

Diagram each argument and answer the question by using an S-W-Slash Chart. Remember, begin by identifying whether each answer choice *strengthens the conclusion, weakens the conclusion,* or *is irrelevant to the conclusion.* Then, eliminate answer choices using your chart.

<u>Note</u>: Problem numbers preceded by "D" refer to questions in the Diagnostic Test chapter of *The Official Guide for GMAT Review, 11th Edition* (pages 32–38).

Strengthen the Conclusion
> *11th Edition:* 7, 9, 13, 16, 19, 26, 28, 30, 36, 37, 41, 43, 53, 54, 63, 69, 73, 100, 103,
>   107, 111, 112, 116, 117, 123, D25, D27, D32
> *Verbal Review:* 1, 3, 22, 25, 31, 33, 35, 36, 53, 55, 69, 70, 76, 80

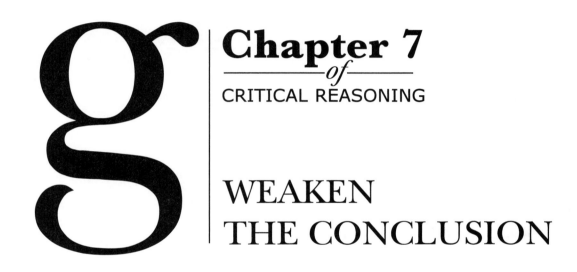

Chapter 7
of
CRITICAL REASONING

WEAKEN
THE CONCLUSION

In This Chapter . . .

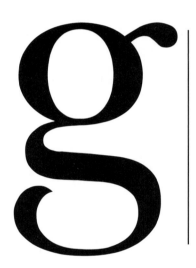

WEAKEN THE CONCLUSION

Weaken the Conclusion questions are among the most common Critical Reasoning questions on the GMAT, appearing slightly more frequently than Strengthen the Conclusion questions.

Weaken the Conclusion questions appear in a number of forms:

> Which of the following, if true, most seriously weakens the argument?

> Which of the following, if true, could present the most serious disadvantage of XYZ Corporation's new marketing initiative?

> Which of the following, if true, most strongly supports the view that the drug treatment program will NOT be successful?

Correct answers do *not* need to make the conclusion false or invalid. Correct answers merely need to make it *less likely* that the stated conclusion is valid.

Almost all correct answers to Weaken The Conclusion questions will **introduce a new piece of evidence that undermines a faulty or tenuous assumption OR that negatively impacts the conclusion directly.**

> To weaken an argument, look for an answer choice that (1) exposes a faulty or tenuous assumption OR (2) negatively impacts the conclusion directly.

Argument/Counterargument

Weaken the Conclusion questions can be made more difficult via a complicated argument structure that contains **two opposing points of view**.

This argument/counterargument structure can also happen within other question types. However, dealing with this more complex structure is particularly challenging on Weaken questions, which already include a reversal. That is, to assess an answer choice for a Weaken question, you must hold it in opposition to the conclusion or to one of its assumptions. When the GMAT adds in the complexity of argument/counterargument, it can become difficult to keep your thoughts straight.

An argument/counterargument structure might look something like this:

> Nicole believes that merging the two divisions will be the best way to improve our company's overall profitability, because the cultures of the two divisions are very similar. However, Nicole is mistaken. Merging the divisions would lead to resentment among employees, as well as redundant personnel and processes.

> Which of the following, if true, would undermine the author's claim that Nicole is incorrect in her belief?

For a confusing question such as this, it is even more important to take notes in an organized fashion. Students who have a confident, robust approach to diagramming will be much better prepared to handle the intricacies of argument/counterargument questions than students who rely only on their short-term memories.

WEAKEN THE CONCLUSION

The first step in attacking this question is to identify the conclusion from the point of view of the AUTHOR. In this case, the author of the argument believes that merging the two divisions is NOT the best way to improve overall profitability.

Next, note the counter-claim, as well as its proponent. The counter-claim is the belief that merging the two divisions IS the best way to improve overall profitability. This belief is held by Nicole. Often, the best way to keep various claims straight is to associate them with their advocates.

Finally, create a modified T-diagram. Extend the central column upward, splitting the area for the conclusion into two sides. Put the author's position on the left side and the counter-claim on the right side. Then fill in the pro's and con's of the <u>author's</u> argument as usual.

For questions involving an argument and a counterargument, the conclusion should be the *author's* position.

Merge ≠ best pln for prof	N: merge = best pln for prof
Empl resent Redund ppl and proc	Similar cultures

The advantage of this method is that it is easy to see the dual role of any piece of evidence. The evidence FOR the author's claim is also opposed to the counter-claim. Likewise, evidence AGAINST the author's claim also supports the counter-claim.

See *The Official Guide, 11th Edition* Question #48 for an example of an argument/counter-argument structure.

The S-W-Slash Chart Revisited

For this question type, we will employ the S-W-Slash chart to organize our process of elimination, as described in the previous chapter of this guide. As you evaluate each answer choice, note down whether each answer

> 1. *strengthens* the conclusion (note with an "**S**"),
> 2. *weakens* the conclusion (note with a "**W**"),
> 3. or is *irrelevant* to the conclusion (note with a "−" or slash-through).

As discussed earlier, you may also note an answer choice that only marginally strengthens or weakens the conclusion with a lowercase "**s**" or "**w**."

Consider the following example:

> The national infrastructure for airport runways and air traffic control requires immediate expansion to accommodate the proliferation of new private, smaller aircraft. The Federal Aviation Authority (the FAA) has proposed a fee for all air travelers to help fund this expansion. However, this fee would be unfair, as it would impose costs on all travelers to benefit only the few who utilize the new private planes.
>
> Which of the following, if true, would allow the FAA to counter the objection that the proposed fee would be unfair?

(A) The existing national airport infrastructure benefits all air travelers.
(B) The fee, if imposed, will have a negligible effect on the overall volume of air travel.
(C) The expansion would reduce the number of delayed flights resulting from small private planes congesting runways.
(D) Travelers who use small private planes are almost uniformly wealthy or traveling on business.
(E) The Administrator of the FAA is appointed by the President, who is subject to national election.

In this argument, the conclusion is that *this fee would be unfair,* with the provided rationale that *it would impose costs on all travelers to benefit only the few who utilize the new private planes.*

Evaluate each of the answer choices using an S-W-Slash chart.

Answer choice (**A**) suggests that the existing infrastructure benefits everyone who would be asked to pay the fee. This seems to speak to the question of fairness. However, the fee itself does not benefit the wide range of air travelers, and it is the fairness of the fee that is in question. This choice is best categorized as irrelevant.

Answer choice (**B**) indicates that the fee will not impact the volume of air travel, implying that the fee will not drive any travelers to stay home or switch to another mode of transportation. This is irrelevant to the conclusion, as a fee can still be unfair even if it does not change behavior.

Answer choice (**C**) weakens the conclusion. If the expansion would reduce delays for all travelers, then all travelers would stand to benefit from the new fee. The issue of fairness is mitigated, since all would benefit in some way from the fee, not only the *few* assumed by the author of the argument.

Answer choice (**D**), if anything, strengthens the conclusion by pointing out that those who use private planes are generally better able to pay a fee than the average traveler. It may be considered unfair to charge the less well-off to benefit those with more resources.

Answer choice (**E**) implies that the fee may be considered fair because the FAA is headed by an individual who is appointed by the President, who is elected. The implication is that any action that stems from the actions of an elected official must be fair. Alternatively, the choice suggests that nothing is unfair since people can elect a new President, who can appoint a new administrator, who can change the fee policy. Notice the large logical leaps required to argue that this answer choice weakens the conclusion. This choice is better classified as irrelevant.

Answer choice (**C**) is the correct answer.

An answer choice that weakens the conclusion without requiring significant leaps of logic is likely correct.

Weaken "EXCEPT" Questions

Consider the following example:

> Supporters of a costly new Defense Advanced Research Projects Agency (DARPA) initiative assert that the project will benefit industrial companies as well as the military itself. In many instances, military research has resulted in technologies that have fueled corporate development and growth, and this pattern can be expected to continue.
>
> Each of the following, if true, serves to weaken the argument above EXCEPT:
>
> (A) The research initiative will occupy many talented scientists, many of whom would otherwise have worked for private corporations.
> (B) In the past decade, DARPA has adopted an increasingly restrictive stance regarding the use of intellectual property resulting from its research.
> (C) A high proportion of the government resources directed toward the initiative would ordinarily have gone to tax subsidies for various businesses.
> (D) The research initiative is focused on materials development through nano-technology, which is thought to have many commercial applications.
> (E) The DARPA research makes use of manufacturing processes that would be cost-prohibitive for most companies to replicate.

In some cases, the correct answer to a Weaken "EXCEPT" question strengthens the conclusion, while in other cases the correct answer is irrelevant to the conclusion.

The conclusion of this argument is that _the project will benefit companies as well as the military._ It is particularly important to use an S-W-slash chart when you are faced with a Strengthen or Weaken question worded in a confusing way, such as this example.

W A
W B
W C
S D
W E

Answer choice (**A**) weakens the conclusion. It indicates that the DARPA initiative will hurt corporations by occupying many talented scientists that would otherwise worked for private companies.

Answer choice (**B**) states that DARPA has been more restrictive in allowing the use of its intellectual property in the last decade. This suggests that, even if commercially useful technologies are developed, companies may not be allowed to benefit. This answer choice weakens the conclusion.

Answer choice (**C**) weakens the conclusion, as the research initiative is shown to hurt businesses by depriving them of tax subsidies.

Answer choice (**D**) strengthens the conclusion. If the research initiative is focused on an area thought to have many commercial applications, the likelihood of businesses benefiting from the research increases.

Answer choice (**E**) weakens the conclusion. If most companies cannot easily replicate the manufacturing processes involved in the research initiative, then it is less reasonable to expect commercial benefits to accrue to businesses as a result.

Answer choice (**D**) is the correct answer.

WEAKEN THE CONCLUSION   **Chapter 7**

Wrong Answer Choice Types

The common categories of wrong answers for Weaken the Conclusion questions are essentially the same as those for Strengthen the Conclusion questions.

A. No Tie to the Conclusion

Many wrong answers are tied to a premise but not to the conclusion. An incorrect answer choice can simply provide unnecessary information about that premise.

Consider again the sample question from earlier in this chapter:

> The national infrastructure for airport runways and air traffic control requires immediate expansion to accommodate the proliferation of new private, smaller aircraft. The Federal Aviation Authority (the FAA) has proposed a fee for all air travelers to help fund this expansion. However, this fee would be unfair, as it would impose costs on all travelers to benefit only the few who utilize the new private planes.
>
> Which of the following, if true, would allow the FAA to counter the objection that the proposed fee would be unfair?

Answer choice (**B**) to the question above is as follows:

> (B) The fee, if imposed, will have a negligible effect on the overall volume of air travel.

This answer choice reveals another consequence of the fee, but it does not address whether the fee will be unfair. Thus, answer choice (**B**) is incorrect.

A few wrong answers with "No Tie to the Conclusion" do bring in language from the conclusion, but they do not meaningfully weaken the conclusion. Deceptive answers such as these <u>seem</u> relevant. Make sure that the answer you choose is not simply related to the conclusion, but in fact weakens it. Consider answer choice (**A**) for the question above:

> (A) The existing national airport infrastructure benefits all air travelers.

Notice how this answer choice relates to fairness (the topic of the conclusion). However, this choice does not actually weaken the conclusion.

Finally, remember that some wrong answers can also be "Real-World Plausible." An answer choice can seem realistic, but you are not assessing its truth or its likelihood in the real world. Only determine whether the choice weakens the argument.

Consider wrong answer choice (**E**) to the question above.

> (E) The Administrator of the FAA is appointed by the President, who is subject to national election.

This answer choice may be true in the real world, but it does not weaken the conclusion.

Wrong answers on EXCEPT versions of Strengthen/Weaken questions are particularly tricky. Take a moment to untangle the knot.

*Manhattan*GMAT°Prep
the new standard
145

B. Wrong Direction

Some wrong answers on Weaken questions in fact strengthen the argument. Make sure that you note whether a particular question is a Weaken the Conclusion or a Strengthen the Conclusion question so that you do not mistakenly pick the wrong answer.

Consider wrong answer choice **(D)** to the question above:

> (D) Travelers who use small private planes are almost uniformly wealthy or traveling on business.

By emphasizing that users of private planes are only a subgroup of all air travelers, this choice actually strengthens the conclusion (that the proposed fee would be unfair).

When you are under test pressure, "Wrong Direction" choices may be very tempting, because they obviously affect the conclusion. An S-W-slash chart can help you avoid making such mistakes.

Be sure not to pick an answer choice that strengthens the conclusion, when you need one that weakens.

Problem Set

Use the skills you have just learned to answer the following Weaken the Conclusion questions. Create an S-W-Slash chart for each set of answer choices. Be sure to diagram each argument. Detailed answers and explanations follow this problem set.

1. Salmon Exports

The United States is considering a ban on the importation of salmon from Country B in order to protest poor protection of intellectual property rights in Country B. An economist counters that such a ban would be ineffective, since Country B would circumvent it by selling the extra salmon in Europe. Indeed, last year, six European nations each imported more salmon than Country B exported to the United States.

Which of the following, if true, would most severely weaken the economist's argument?

(A) Salmon is the chief export of Country B, accounting for a substantial proportion of its export earnings over each of the last three years.
(B) The supply of native salmon has become increasingly limited in certain parts of North America in the past decade, including many parts of the United States.
(C) Salmon from Country B is considered a delicacy in all of the European nations that imported salmon last year.
(D) The economic value to U.S. companies of the adoption of intellectual property regulations in Country B is greater than the value of salmon exports from Country B.
(E) Costs for the transportation of salmon from Country B to Europe would make salmon from Country B more expensive for European consumers than salmon imported from other countries.

2.Coconut Fun Snax

At Hospital A, there has been an upsurge in emergency room visits by children under twelve with stomach disturbances. Patient tracking revealed that the vast majority of the children had eaten candy labeled "Coconut Fun Snax" shortly before the onset of symptoms. The emergency room physicians concluded that it is unsafe for children under the age of twelve to eat products containing coconut.

Which of the following, if true, would be the best reason to doubt the warning?

(A) Coconuts contain saturated fats.
(B) Some pathogens are not detectable by any medical tests.
(C) No coconuts or coconut products are used in the manufacture of "Coconut Fun Snax."
(D) The patient tracking at the hospital contacted the parents of all of the children concerned and received full cooperation from them.
(E) Coconuts are a favorite food of many children.

3. Smithtown Theatre

The Smithtown Theatre, a town theatre that stages old Broadway shows, has announced a new expansion that will substantially increase both the capacity and the costs of operating the theatre. Attendance at the Smithtown Theatre is currently just enough for the theatre to cover its

*Manhattan*GMAT*Prep

present operating costs. In addition, all of the current patrons of the theatre live in Smithtown, and the population of the town is not expected to increase in the next several years. Thus, it seems certain that the expansion of the Smithtown Theatre will prove unprofitable.

Which of the following, if true, would most seriously weaken the argument?

(A) A large movie chain plans to open a new multiplex location in Smithtown later this year.
(B) Concession sales in the Smithtown Theatre comprise a substantial proportion of the theatre's revenues.
(C) Many recent arrivals to Smithtown are students that are less likely to attend the Smithtown Theatre than are older residents.
(D) The expansion would allow the Smithtown Theatre to stage larger, more popular shows that will attract patrons from neighboring towns.
(E) The Board of the Smithtown Theatre responsible for choosing which shows to stage regularly solicits input from residents of the town.

4. Books and Coffee
The respective owners of a book store and a coffee shop that are next door to one another have decided to combine their businesses. Both owners believe that this merger will help increase the number of customers, and therefore the gross revenue. They reason that customers who come for a cup of coffee might find themselves glancing at the book titles for sale, and those who come for books might like to sit down and start reading with a cup of coffee.

Which of the following, if true, most weakens the owners' conclusion that a merger will increase revenue?

(A) Books and drinks can both be considered impulse purchases; often, they are purchased by customers without forethought.
(B) Because of the way in which the two stores are currently positioned relative to one another, many customers who come to the coffee shop never see or notice the book store.
(C) If books are damaged in a bookstore before purchase, the customers responsible for the damage are generally not held financially accountable.
(D) The coffee shop is primarily frequented by local high school students whose parents make up a large percentage of the book store's customer base; the teenagers use the coffee shop as a place to mingle with their friends without family involvement.
(E) A combination book store and coffee shop that opened in a neighboring city last year has already earned higher than expected profits.

5. Band Popularity
A recent article asserted that, from 2002 to 2006, Band 1 generated the most revenue of any band in the world. The article based this claim on the fact that in each of those years, Band 1 sold the most albums, and Band 1's highly anticipated first concert tour was the highest grossing concert tour in the industry in 2006.

Which of the following, if true, weakens the article's assertion?

(A) The band with the highest grossing tour in the industry in 2002 did not tour again in the next four years.
(B) Band 1 typically puts on extraordinarily expensive concerts with elaborate staging, video displays and light shows.
(C) From 2002 to 2006, other bands released concert film and video anthology DVDs that were extremely lucrative.
(D) All of Band 1's albums released from 2002 to 2006 were poorly received by music critics.
(E) Internet piracy of music resulted in depressed album sales for the period 2002 to 2006 relative to earlier years.

6. Half-Price Passes

A nonprofit organization in Motor City has proposed that local college students be given the option to buy half-price monthly passes for the city's public transportation system. The non-profit claims that this plan will reduce air pollution in Motor City while increasing profits for the city's public transportation system. However, this plan is unlikely to meet its goals, as

_____.

Which of the following most logically completes the argument above?

(A) most college students in Motor City view public transportation as unsafe
(B) most college students in Motor City view public transportation as prohibitively expensive
(C) college students typically do not have the 9-to-5 schedules of most workers, and can thus be expected to ride public transportation at times when there are plenty of empty seats
(D) a bus produces more air pollution per mile than does a car
(E) a large proportion of the college students in Motor City live off campus

7. Ethanol

Ethanol, a fuel derived from corn, can be used alone to power automobiles equipped with special engines or as an additive to gasoline to reduce the consumption of fossil fuels in petroleum engines. Unlike fossil fuels, ethanol is a sustainable fuel since it is primarily the result of the conversion of the sun's energy into usable energy. Moreover, compared with conventional unleaded gasoline, pure ethanol is a cleaner burning fuel that combusts with oxygen to form carbon dioxide and water. Thus, many individuals advocate the increased usage of ethanol as a primary fuel source in conjunction with or in place of gasoline in the United States.

Each of the following, if true, undermines the usage of ethanol as a primary fuel source EXCEPT:

(A) The energy required to grow and process the corn used as fuel is greater than the amount of energy ultimately produced.
(B) Corn grown for fuel would not require as much pesticide usage as corn grown for food, since consumer reaction to food appearance is a major contributor to the prolific use of pesticides.
(C) Ethanol is more expensive to produce than gasoline and furnishes fewer miles per gallon.
(D) If the entire annual U.S. harvest of corn were devoted exclusively to ethanol production to replace gasoline, the ethanol produced would cover twelve days of typical US gasoline consumption.

*Manhattan*GMAT*Prep*

(E) Ethanol used as a gasoline additive produces volatile organic compounds that react with sunlight to form ozone and produce smog.

8. Merit Pay

Traditionally, public school instructors have been compensated according to seniority. Recently, the existing salary system has been increasingly criticized as an approach to compensation that rewards lackadaisical teaching and punishes motivated, highly-qualified instruction. Instead, educational experts argue that, to retain exceptional teachers and maintain quality instruction, teachers should receive salaries or bonuses based on performance rather than seniority.

Which of the following, if true, most weakens the argument of the educational experts?

(A) Some teachers express that financial compensation is not the only factor contributing to job satisfaction and teaching performance.
(B) School districts will develop their own unique compensation structures that may differ greatly from those of other school districts.
(C) Upon leaving the teaching profession, many young, effective teachers cite a lack of opportunity for more rapid financial advancement as a primary factor in the decision to change careers.
(D) A merit-based system that bases compensation on teacher performance reduces collaboration, which is an integral component of quality instruction.
(E) In school districts that have implemented pay for performance compensation structures, standardized test scores have dramatically increased.

9. APR

Company Spokesperson: Over the past several years, our company has more than doubled its revenues within the credit card division. However, over the same period, the division's profits have steadily declined, largely as a result of a rapid increase in default rates on credit card loans among our customers. It is time to recognize that our previous strategy was flawed, since we failed to increase the average annual percentage rate (APR) charged on outstanding balances to compensate for the higher default rates. According to our estimates, increasing the interest charged on outstanding balances from an APR of 9.5% to an APR of 12% will be sufficient to compensate for the current rate of defaults and bring the division back to profitable growth.

Which of the following statements would most seriously undermine a plan to increase interest rates in order to spur profitable growth?

(A) Many other companies have experienced a similar trend in their default rates.
(B) The company's operating expenses are above the industry average and can be substantially reduced, thus increasing margins.
(C) The rapid increase in default rates was due to a rise in unemployment, but unemployment rates are expected to drop in the coming months.
(D) The proposed increase in the APR will, alone, more than double the company's operating margins.
(E) An increase in the APR charged on credit card balances often results in higher rates of default.

ManhattanGMAT Prep
the new standard

10. Holographic Displays

Displayco is marketing a holographic display to supermarkets that shows three-dimensional images of certain packaged goods in the aisles. Displayco's marketing literature states that patrons at supermarkets will be strongly attracted to goods that are promoted in this way, resulting in higher profits for the supermarkets that purchase the displays. Consumer advocates, however, feel that the displays will be intrusive to supermarket patrons and may even increase minor accidents involving shopping carts.

Which of the following, if true, most seriously weakens the position of the consumer advocates?

(A) The holographic displays are expensive to install and maintain.

(B) Many other venues, including shopping malls, are considering adopting holographic displays.

(C) Accidents in supermarkets that are serious enough to cause injury are rare.

(D) Supermarkets tend to be low-margin businesses that struggle to achieve profitability.

(E) Studies in test markets have shown that supermarket patrons quickly become accustomed to holographic displays.

1. Salmon Exports

The United States is considering a ban on the importation of salmon from Country B in order to protest poor protection of intellectual property rights in Country B. An economist counters that such a ban would be ineffective, since Country B would circumvent it by selling the extra salmon in Europe. Indeed, last year, six European nations each imported more salmon than Country B exported to the United States.

Which of the following, if true, would most severely weaken the economist's argument?

(A) Salmon is the chief export of Country B, accounting for a substantial proportion of its export earnings over each of the last three years.

(B) The supply of native salmon has become increasingly limited in certain parts of North America in the past decade, including many parts of the United States.

(C) Salmon from Country B is considered a delicacy in all of the European nations that imported salmon last year.

(D) The economic value to U.S. companies of the adoption of intellectual property regulations in Country B is greater than the value of salmon exports from Country B.

(E) Costs for the transportation of salmon from Country B to Europe would make salmon from Country B more expensive for European consumers than salmon imported from other countries.

This argument concerns a claim from an economist over the use of sanctions to pressure the government of Country B into adopting certain regulations. The economist claims that the ban will not work because Country B can simply circumvent the sanctions from the United States by increasing exports to Europe. The question asks which answer choice would most weaken the economist's position. The correct answer choice will demonstrate that Country B would not be able to easily circumvent the sanctions by increasing salmon exports to Europe.

(A) Strengthen/irrelevant. If salmon exports represent a substantial proportion of the exports of Country B, it seems more likely that the sanctions may have some serious impact; Country B may not be able to increase exports to Europe enough to offset the loss in the US. This answer choice could also be considered irrelevant, as it still leaves open the possibility that Country B would simply increase exports to Europe in response to the sanctions.

(B) Irrelevant. This information does not affect the ability of Country B to increase its exports to Europe in response to sanctions from the United States. It does suggest that the United States might not benefit greatly from imposing sanctions, as it could face a limited supply of salmon unless it imports from another country, but the question asks us to weaken the economist's claim.

(C) Strengthen. Such a condition would support the economist's contention, since it demonstrates the existence of a European market for salmon from Country B, and potentially even the possibility that Country B can charge a premium for its salmon.

(D) Irrelevant. The relative value of the intellectual property regulations and the salmon exports from Country B do not impact the ability of Country B to circumvent sanctions by increasing its exports to Europe.

(E) CORRECT. Weaken. The additional costs of transportation to Europe would make salmon from Country B more expensive for European consumers than salmon from other sources. This piece of information makes it less likely that Country B will be able to offset decreased exports to the United States with increased exports to Europe, casting doubt on the economist's claim.

2. Coconut Fun Snax

At Hospital A, there has been an upsurge in emergency room visits by children under twelve with stomach disturbances. Patient tracking revealed that the vast majority of the children had eaten candy labeled "Coconut Fun Snax" shortly before the onset of symptoms. The emergency room physicians concluded that it is unsafe for children under the age of twelve to eat products containing coconut.

Which of the following, if true, would be the best reason to doubt the warning?

(A) Coconuts contain saturated fats.
(B) Some pathogens are not detectable by any medical tests.
(C) No coconuts or coconut products are used in the manufacture of "Coconut Fun Snax."
(D) The patient tracking at the hospital contacted the parents of all of the children concerned and received full cooperation from them.
(E) Coconuts are a favorite food of many children.

This question asks for the choice that weakens the conclusion that children under the age of twelve should not consume products containing coconut. The doctors' warning was based on the information that vast majority of children suffering from stomach disturbances ate Coconut Fun Snax shortly before becoming ill.

(A) Irrelevant. In the real world, we may know that saturated fats are supposed to be unhealthy, but unhealthy is not the same thing as unsafe. In addition, the argument does not actually tell us that saturated fats are unhealthy; we are not supposed to need real-world knowledge of a subject in order to answer the question.

(B) Irrelevant. This may be true but it does not weaken the specific conclusion that coconut is unsafe for children under the age of twelve.

(C) CORRECT. Weaken. The conclusion was based on data about children who had eaten "Coconut Fun Snax". If "Coconut Fun Snax" do not actually contain coconut, the premises do not support the doctors' warning.

(D) Strengthen/Irrelevant. If every parent was contacted and cooperated fully, this would increase the quality of the patient tracking data cited in the premise. Establishing that an argument's premises rest on sound data tends to strengthen the argument overall. At best, this information is irrelevant to the specific conclusion here.

(E) Irrelevant. The fact that children may enjoy a particular food provides no assurance that the food is, or is not, consistently safe for children under a certain age.

3. Smithtown Theatre

The Smithtown Theatre, a town theatre that stages old Broadway shows, has announced a new expansion that will substantially increase both the capacity and the costs of operating the theatre. Attendance at the Smithtown Theatre is currently just enough for the theatre to cover its present operating costs. In addition, all of the current patrons of the theatre live in Smithtown, and the population of the town is not expected to increase in the next several years. Thus, it seems certain that the expansion of the Smithtown Theatre will prove unprofitable.

Which of the following, if true, would most seriously weaken the argument?

(A) A large movie chain plans to open a new multiplex location in Smithtown later this year.
(B) Concession sales in the Smithtown Theatre comprise a substantial proportion of the theatre's revenues.
(C) Many recent arrivals to Smithtown are students that are less likely to attend the Smithtown Theatre than are older residents.
(D) The expansion would allow the Smithtown Theatre to stage larger, more popular shows that will attract patrons from neighboring towns.
(E) The Board of the Smithtown Theatre responsible for choosing which shows to stage regularly solicits input from residents of the town.

The argument describes the expansion of a town theatre. The theatre currently breaks even, and the town in which the theatre operates is not growing. The argument concludes that the expansion of the Smithtown Theatre will prove to be unprofitable. The question asks which answer choice weakens the conclusion; thus, the correct answer choice will present a reason why, despite the current situation, the planned expansion will prove to be profitable.

(A) Strengthen / irrelevant. If a large movie chain were to open a new multiplex location in Smithtown, the residents of Smithtown would have at least one more choice as to how to spend an evening's entertainment. If anything, this would negatively impact the profitability of the expansion of the Smithtown Theatre; at best, this choice would be irrelevant.

(B) Irrelevant. The fact that concession sales are a substantial proportion of the revenue generated by Smithtown Theatre is irrelevant to the argument. It is established in the premises that the Smithtown Theatre currently generates only enough revenue to break even, regardless of how that revenue is generated.

(C) Strengthen. The influx of students who are unlikely to attend the Smithtown Theatre further reinforces the idea that the expansion of the theatre is likely to be unprofitable.

(D) CORRECT. Weaken. If the expansion will allow the Smithtown Theatre to stage larger shows that will attract patrons from nearby towns, then the expansion may turn out to be profitable. Note that this does not conflict with the premises, which describe the current population of patrons of the theatre before the proposed expansion.

(E) Irrelevant. The fact that the Board of the Smithtown Theatre solicits input from residents of the town does not affect the expected profitability of the proposed expansion of the theatre.

4. Books and Coffee

The respective owners of a book store and a coffee shop that are next door to one another have decided to combine their businesses. Both owners believe that this merger will help increase the number of customers, and therefore the gross revenue. They reason that customers who come for a cup of coffee might find themselves glancing at the book titles for sale, and those who come for books might like to sit down and start reading with a cup of coffee.

Which of the following, if true, most weakens the owners' conclusion that a merger will increase revenue?

(A) Books and drinks can both be considered impulse purchases; often, they are purchased by customers without forethought.
(B) Because of the way in which the two stores are currently positioned relative to one another, many customers who come to the coffee shop never see or notice the book store.
(C) If books are damaged in a bookstore store before purchase, the customers responsible for the damage are generally not held financially accountable.
(D) The coffee shop is primarily frequented by local high school students whose parents make up a large percentage of the book store's customer base; the teenagers use the coffee shop as a place to mingle with their friends without family involvement.
(E) A combination book store and coffee shop that opened in a neighboring city last year has already earned higher than expected profits.

The owners believe that the merger will produce more customers, which in turn will create higher revenue. The correct answer will give reason to doubt that the merger will result in higher revenue.

(A) **Strengthen.** This answer choice validates the claim that those who come in to buy coffee might buy books, and those who come in for books might suddenly decide to buy coffee.

(B) **Strengthen.** If the two stores are combined, coffee customers who did not notice the books for sale earlier will notice them now, and if some purchase books, revenue will increase.

(C) **Irrelevant.** This statement has no direct relationship with the conclusion which discusses revenue, not profits. We do not have any information to determine whether combining the two stores will increase, decrease, or do nothing to the frequency with which books are damaged within the store.

(D) CORRECT. Weaken. If teenagers frequent the coffee shop in order to get away from their parents, and if their parents are now going to be coming to the combined coffee shop and book store, the teenagers may stop coming to the coffee shop as a result. This would shrink the combined customer base, and thus this answer choice weakens the conclusion.

(E) **Irrelevant.** This statement has no direct relationship with the conclusion. There are too many unknown factors about the store in the neighboring city, and not enough to connect what happened in that store with what will happen in this one. If similar factors could be established, then this choice might strengthen the conclusion.

5. Band Popularity

A recent article asserted that, from 2002 to 2006, Band 1 generated the most revenue of any band in the world. The article based this claim on the fact that in each of those years, Band 1 sold the most albums, and Band 1's highly anticipated first concert tour was the highest grossing concert tour in the industry in 2006.

Which of the following, if true, weakens the article's assertion?

(A) The band with the highest grossing tour in the industry in 2002 did not tour again in the next four years.
(B) Band 1 typically puts on extraordinarily expensive concerts with elaborate staging, video displays and light shows.
(C) From 2002 to 2006, other bands released concert film and video anthology DVDs that were extremely lucrative.
(D) All of Band 1's albums released from 2002 to 2006 were poorly received by music critics.
(E) Internet piracy of music resulted in depressed album sales for the period 2002 to 2006 relative to earlier years.

The article claims that Band 1 generated the most revenue of any band during the period 2002 to 2006. The evidence presented is that Band 1 sold the most albums in each of those years, and had the top grossing tour in 2006. This conclusion would be weakened if there were substantial sources of revenue for bands other than album sales and tours during the period. Alternatively, another band might have toured more often than Band 1 for the period 2002 through 2006, or earned more from touring in the years 2002 through 2005.

(A) Strengthen/irrelevant. If the band that had the highest grossing tour in 2002 did not tour again during the period in question, it may be more likely that Band 1 did generate more revenue than other bands during that period. At best, this is irrelevant to the claim that Band 1 generated the most revenue during the period 2002 to 2006.

(B) Irrelevant. The fact that the concerts put on by Band 1 were extraordinarily expensive does not impact the revenue generated by the band during the period. It may influence tour profitability, but that is beyond the scope of this argument.

(C) CORRECT. Weaken. The evidence presented for the claim that Band 1 generated the most revenue in the period 2002 to 2006 on a revenue basis relies on album sales and concert tours. However, if other bands released very lucrative DVDs during this period, another band may have generated more revenue overall than did Band 1, which apparently did not release lucrative DVDs (the choice says that "other bands" did this, not Band 1).

(D) Irrelevant. The reception of music critics to Band 1's albums is irrelevant to the amount of revenue generated by the band in the period, as given by the premises.

(E) Irrelevant. The fact that album sales were depressed from 2002 to 2006 does not affect whether Band 1 generated the most revenue in the period. Other bands would face the same threat of piracy.

6. Half-Price Passes

A nonprofit organization in Motor City has proposed that local college students be given the option to buy half-price monthly passes for the city's public transportation system. The nonprofit claims that this plan will reduce air pollution in Motor City while increasing profits for the city's public transportation system. However, this plan is unlikely to meet its goals, as _____.

Which of the following most logically completes the argument above?

(A) most college students in Motor City view public transportation as unsafe
(B) most college students in Motor City view public transportation as prohibitively expensive
(C) college students typically do not have the 9-to-5 schedules of most workers, and can thus be expected to ride public transportation at times when there are plenty of empty seats
(D) a bus produces more air pollution per mile than does a car
(E) a large proportion of the college students in Motor City live off campus

The nonprofit organization claims that allowing students to buy half-price monthly passes will reduce air pollution and increase profits for the public transportation system. For this plan to be sound, it must be true that: (1) students will respond to the price incentive by buying more monthly passes, and (2) increased student ridership will reduce air pollution and increase profits. To find a consideration that would weaken the argument for this plan, look for a statement that casts some doubt on (1) or (2).

(A) CORRECT. Weaken. If students perceive public transportation as unsafe, it is unlikely that they will want to increase their use of public transportation, even at a discount. This answer choice undermines claim (1) above.

(B) Strengthen. If a high price is currently deterring students from riding public transportation, it is likely that a 50% price cut will increase student ridership—just as the nonprofit claims.

(C) Strengthen. If college students' schedules are such that the students can be expected to ride public transportation at times when there are plenty of empty seats available, we can expect that the public transportation system will be able to collect revenue from the students without having to significantly increase the number of buses and trains in operation. Extra revenue with minimal extra cost typically means extra profit, which is what the nonprofit predicts.

(D) Irrelevant. This might seem to undermine claim (2), that the half-price plan will reduce air pollution. However, this comparison between pollution per mile from buses and cars is not helpful because a bus carries many more people at one time than does a car.

(E) Irrelevant. If a large proportion of the students in Motor City live off campus, they presumably need some form of transportation to get between home and campus. We are given no information, however, to determine whether students will prefer public or private transportation.

7. Ethanol

Ethanol, a fuel derived from corn, can be used alone to power automobiles equipped with special engines or as an additive to gasoline to reduce the consumption of fossil fuels in petroleum engines. Unlike fossil fuels, ethanol is a sustainable fuel since it is primarily the result of the conversion of the sun's energy into usable energy. Moreover, compared with conventional unleaded gasoline, pure ethanol is a cleaner burning fuel that combusts with oxygen to form carbon dioxide and water. Thus, many individuals advocate the increased usage of ethanol as a primary fuel source in conjunction with or in place of gasoline in the United States.

Each of the following, if true, undermines the usage of ethanol as a primary fuel source EXCEPT:

(A) The energy required to grow and process the corn used as fuel is greater than the amount of energy ultimately produced.

(B) Corn grown for fuel would not require as much pesticide usage as corn grown for food, since consumer reaction to food appearance is a major contributor to the prolific use of pesticides.

(C) Ethanol is more expensive to produce than gasoline and furnishes fewer miles per gallon.

(D) If the entire annual U.S. harvest of corn were devoted exclusively to ethanol production to replace gasoline, the ethanol produced would cover twelve days of typical US gasoline consumption.

(E) Ethanol used as a gasoline additive produces volatile organic compounds that react with sunlight to form ozone and produce smog.

The argument is concerned with the use of corn-derived ethanol as a fuel source. According to the text, ethanol is a sustainable fuel source that burns more cleanly than conventional gasoline. The question indicates that four of the answer choices will undermine, or weaken, the claim that ethanol should be used as a primary fuel source and one answer choice (the correct one) will NOT weaken the claim.

(A) Weaken. This choice indicates that the amount of energy needed to process the corn into fuel is greater than the amount of energy produced. In other words, using ethanol would result in a net loss of energy.

(B) CORRECT. Irrelevant. This statement indicates that corn grown for ethanol would need less pesticide than corn grown for food. This does not impact the claim that we should use ethanol as a primary fuel source, presumably in place of fossil fuels.

(C) Weaken. It is less likely that ethanol would be adopted as a primary fuel source in place of gasoline if ethanol is more expensive to produce than gasoline and furnishes fewer miles per gallon.

(D) Weaken. This choice indicates that there simply is not enough corn available to permit ethanol to become a primary source of fuel in place of gasoline.

(E) Weaken. Although pure ethanol burns more cleanly than conventional gasoline, this choice indicates that ethanol, when used as an additive, creates compounds that are detrimental to the environment.

8. Merit Pay

Traditionally, public school instructors have been compensated according to seniority. Recently, the existing salary system has been increasingly criticized as an approach to compensation that rewards lackadaisical teaching and punishes motivated, highly-qualified instruction. Instead, educational experts argue that, to retain exceptional teachers and maintain quality instruction, teachers should receive salaries or bonuses based on performance rather than seniority.

Which of the following, if true, most weakens the conclusion of the educational experts?

(A) Some teachers express that financial compensation is not the only factor contributing to job satisfaction and teaching performance.

(B) School districts will develop their own unique compensation structures that may differ greatly from those of other school districts.

(C) Upon leaving the teaching profession, many young, effective teachers cite a lack of opportunity for more rapid financial advancement as a primary factor in the decision to change careers.

(D) A merit-based system that bases compensation on teacher performance reduces collaboration, which is an integral component of quality instruction.

(E) In school districts that have implemented pay for performance compensation structures, standardized test scores have dramatically increased.

The argument is concerned with how public school teachers are compensated. It suggests that educational experts believe that a system of teacher compensation based on performance rather than seniority would help to retain exceptional teachers and maintain quality instruction. The correct answer is the one that most undermines this contention of the educational experts.

(A) Irrelevant. The fact that other factors also contribute to job satisfaction and teaching performance neither weakens nor strengthens the argument for a performance-based pay structure for public school teachers.

(B) Irrelevant. Nothing in the argument indicates that one universal system of compensation must be adopted in order to implement this plan. It is very possible that several effective models of performance-based pay could be developed and implemented successfully.

(C) Strengthen. This choice indicates that many young, effective teachers are extremely frustrated by the traditional pay structure, in which financial advancement is directly tied to seniority. Thus, these teachers would likely welcome a change that allows them more rapid opportunity for financial advancement.

(D) **CORRECT.** Weaken. This choice indicates that collaboration among teachers is integral to high-quality instruction and that a system of compensation based on teacher performance reduces collaboration. Thus, the effect of a merit-based system of pay would be to undermine quality instruction, which is one of the two stated goals of the educational experts.

(E) Strengthen. The educational experts' argument in favor of performance-based compensation is bolstered if standardized tests scores have dramatically risen in school districts that have instituted such pay structures.

9. APR

Company Spokesperson: Over the past several years, our company has more than doubled its revenues within the credit card division. However, over the same period, the division's profits have steadily declined, largely as a result of a rapid increase in default rates on credit card loans among our customers. It is time to recognize that our previous strategy was flawed, since we failed to increase the average annual percentage rate (APR) charged on outstanding balances to compensate for the higher default rates. According to our estimates, increasing the interest charged on outstanding balances from an APR of 9.5% to an APR of 12% will be sufficient to compensate for the current rate of defaults and bring the division back to profitable growth.

Which of the following statements would most seriously undermine a plan to increase interest rates in order to spur profitable growth?

(A) Many other companies have experienced a similar trend in their default rates.
(B) The company's operating expenses are above the industry average and can be substantially reduced, thus increasing margins.
(C) The rapid increase in default rates was due to a rise in unemployment, but unemployment rates are expected to drop in the coming months.
(D) The proposed increase in the APR will, alone, more than double the company's operating margins.
(E) An increase in the APR charged on credit card balances often results in higher rates of default.

In the above argument, the spokesperson cites the evidence that the increases in the company's revenues have been associated with a rapid decline in profits. The spokesperson attributes this poor performance to higher default rates and a lack of corresponding increases in interest rates charged by the company. The question asks us to weaken a plan to spur profitable growth by increasing interest rates.

(A) Irrelevant. The fact that other companies have also experienced a rising default rate does not impact the plan to improve profitability by raising interest rates.

(B) Irrelevant. While this answer choice demonstrates that there exist other opportunities to increase the company's profitability, it does not weaken the claim that raising interest rates will increase profitability.

(C) Irrelevant. This choice explains why default rates rose and gives some reason to believe that default rates might drop in the near future. This does not weaken the claim, however, that raising interest rates will increase profitability.

(D) Strengthen. This answer choice demonstrates that the proposed strategy is likely to achieve its main purpose of improving profitability and thus strengthens rather than weakens the conclusion.

(E) CORRECT. Weaken. This answer choice indicates that the suggested strategy may result in an even higher rate of default, which would exacerbate rather than solve the problem.

10. Holographic Displays

Displayco is marketing a holographic display to supermarkets that shows three-dimensional images of certain packaged goods in the aisles. Displayco's marketing literature states that patrons at supermarkets will be strongly attracted to goods that are promoted in this way, resulting in higher profits for the supermarkets that purchase the displays. Consumer advocates, however, feel that the displays will be intrusive to supermarket patrons and may even increase minor accidents involving shopping carts.

Which of the following, if true, most seriously weakens the position of the consumer advocates?

(A) The holographic displays are expensive to install and maintain.
(B) Many other venues, including shopping malls, are considering adopting holographic displays.
(C) Accidents in supermarkets that are serious enough to cause injury are rare.
(D) Supermarkets tend to be low-margin businesses that struggle to achieve profitability.
(E) Studies in test markets have shown that supermarket patrons quickly become accustomed to holographic displays.

This problem contains both an argument and a counter-argument. The first argument is articulated by Displayco, which argues that holographic displays will attract supermarket patrons and increase supermarket profits. The counter-argument is voiced by consumer advocates, who hold that the holographic displays will be intrusive to customers and may even increase minor accidents. We are asked to weaken the second argument; thus, the correct answer choice will suggest that the concerns presented by the consumer advocates are not problematic.

(A) Irrelevant. This answer choice may weaken the argument of Displayco, but we were asked to weaken the consumer advocates' argument. This choice does not influence whether patrons will find the displays intrusive and distracting.

(B) Irrelevant. The potential adoption of holographic displays by other venues does not impact the concerns of consumer advocates that the displays will be intrusive and distracting. It could be the case that holographic displays will be intrusive and distracting in all of these other venues as well.

(C) Irrelevant. One might think that this answer choice would weaken the consumer advocates' argument. However, the consumer advocates' argument did not use the standard of "causing injury" as a threshold for minor accidents. Minor accidents can be bothersome to patrons without causing injury.

(D) Irrelevant. While this choice might help Displayco to convince supermarkets to use its product, we were asked to weaken the consumer advocates' concerns. The struggles of supermarkets to achieve profitability is not relevant to the consumer advocates' concerns.

(E) CORRECT. If studies in test markets have shown that patrons quickly become accustomed to holographic displays, then patrons are much less likely to find the displays intrusive after an initial adjustment period. Further, if patrons become used to the displays, the displays are unlikely to increase the frequency of minor accidents involving shopping carts.

*Manhattan*GMAT*Prep
the new standard

REAL GMAT PROBLEMS

Now that you have completed your study of WEAKEN THE CONCLUSION questions, it is time to test your skills on passages that have actually appeared on real GMAT exams over the past several years.

The problem set below is composed of Critical Reasoning passages from two books published by GMAC (Graduate Management Admission Council):

The Official Guide for GMAT Review, 11th Edition (pages 32–38 & 468–504)
The Official Guide for GMAT Verbal Review (pages 116–142)

Diagram each argument and answer the question by using an S-W-Slash Chart. Remember, begin by identifying whether each answer choice *strengthens the conclusion, weakens the conclusion, or neither strengthens nor weakens the conclusion*. Then, eliminate answer choices using your chart.

Note: Problem numbers preceded by "D" refer to questions in the Diagnostic Test chapter of *The Official Guide for GMAT Review, 11th Edition* (pages 32–38).

Weaken the Conclusion

> *11th Edition:* 1, 3, 5, 10, 12, 15, 17, 18, 20, 23, 27, 33, 38, 39, 40, 42, 44, 48, 55, 61, 62, 64, 65, 67, 68, 72, 78, 79, 83, 84, 85, 86, 88, 91, 93, 98, 102, 113, 114, 115, 118, 120, 121, 122, 124, D18, D20, D23, D26, D30, D34
>
> *Verbal Review:* 4, 6, 11, 15, 16, 17, 18, 19, 21, 24, 26, 27, 28, 29, 32, 37, 39, 40, 46, 47, 48, 49, 50, 54, 60, 68, 71, 79, 81

Chapter 8
of
CRITICAL REASONING

MINOR
QUESTION TYPES

In This Chapter . . .

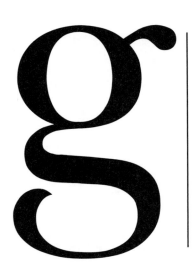

- Explain an Event or Discrepancy
- Analyze the Argument Structure
- Evaluate the Conclusion
- Resolve a Problem
- Provide an Example
- Restate the Conclusion
- Mimic the Argument

Minor Question Types

Aside from the four major types of Critical Reasoning questions discussed in preceding chapters, several *minor* types can appear on the GMAT. You will probably see two to three questions from all the minor types combined, and no more than one question of any particular minor type. In contrast, you are likely to see two to three questions of each of the four major types. As a result, you should spend less study time on the minor types.

Examples of each of these minor question types appear in the problem set at the end of this chapter. The types are presented in approximate order of importance.

1. Explain an Event or Discrepancy

You may see a few questions of these minor types on your exam.

This is the most common of the minor question types. The question generally poses two seemingly contradictory premises and asks you to find the answer choice that best reconciles them. The question will often, though not always, indicate what the discrepancy is or provide a keyword pointing to the discrepancy in the argument. For example:

> Which of the following statements, if true, would best explain the sudden drop in temperature?

> Which of the following, if true, most helps to resolve the paradox described above?

Like Draw a Conclusion arguments, Explain an Event arguments will contain only premises. There will be no conclusion in the argument. You will be told that the information provided is somehow puzzling or contradictory via signals such as *yet, however, nonetheless,* or *paradoxically*. You may also be given a more explicit signal such as *the results are surprising because....*

To solve Explain an Event problems, look for the answer choice that provides a new, fact-based premise that directly illustrates why the apparent discrepancy is not a discrepancy after all. The correct answer will often contain some very specific new piece of information that resolves the given discrepancy. You might not have anticipated this information ahead of time, but after you add it to the existing premises, the situation should make sense. In this respect, questions of this type are similar to logic gap questions discussed in the "Find the Assumption" chapter. In both cases, the correct answer fills a logical hole in the argument.

Consider the following example:

> In a recent poll, 71% of respondents reported that they cast votes in the most recent national election. Voting records show, however, that only 60% of eligible voters actually voted in that election.

> Which of the following pieces of evidence, if true, would provide the best explanation for the discrepancy?

(A) The margin of error for the survey was plus or minus five percentage points.
(B) Fifteen percent of the survey's respondents were living overseas at the time of the election.
(C) Prior research has shown that people who actually do vote are also more likely to respond to polls than those who do not vote.
(D) Some people who intend to vote are prevented from doing so by last-minute conflicts on election day or other complications.
(E) Polls about voting behavior typically have margins of error within plus or minus three percentage points.

For Explain an Event or Discrepancy questions, choose an answer that allows all the premises to be true without any perceived conflict.

The argument consists entirely of factual premises. The facts in the first sentence appear to contradict the facts in the second sentence. The correct answer will provide a new premise that resolves this apparent discrepancy.

Answer choice **(A)** begins promisingly by discussing a margin of error. The choice does not go far enough. A margin of error of 5 percentage points will not close the 11 percentage point gap between the two statistics in the argument.

Answer choice **(B)** mentions a percentage larger than the 11 point discrepancy in the argument. The percentage, however, applies to the percentage of respondents living overseas at the time of the election. This 15% could be part of the group that did not vote, or these people could have voted by absentee ballot, or we could have some mix of the two. In any event, this does not give us enough information to resolve the discrepancy.

Answer choice **(C)** provides a reason why a higher percentage of the poll respondents said that they voted than eligible voters actually voted. If those voters are also more likely to respond to polls, then they will be over-represented in the poll numbers.

While answer choice **(D)** may be true, it does not explain the discrepancy in the statistics presented in the argument. The poll asked about voters' actual actions during the last election, not what they intended to do.

Answer choice **(E)** may also be true, but it does not explain the discrepancy in the statistics presented in the argument. Even after adjusting for a three percent margin of error, the statistics are substantially different.

A common wrong answer type will typically discuss one of the premises but not actually address the discrepancy between conflicting premises. Choices **(A)**, **(B)**, and **(D)** fall into this category.

Another common wrong answer type is Wrong Direction. A choice of this type will support the fact that the discrepancy exists, rather than explaining why there is not actually a discrepancy after all. Choice **(E)**, above, falls into this category. Be careful not to misread the question and think that we are supposed to explain why the apparent discrepancy <u>exists</u>. Remember that this is not what we are supposed to do on problems of this type. Rather, we must explain why the apparent discrepancy is *not* a real discrepancy.

2. Analyze the Argument Structure

Analyze the Argument Structure questions ask you to describe the role of a part or parts of the argument. Unfortunately, the arguments tend to be complex, often with an argument/counterargument structure. You should thus use a modified-T diagram to take notes.

Although this type is not as common as Explain an Event or Discrepancy, you should know that Analyze Structure questions are very challenging and tend to be overly time-consuming. You should be ready to eliminate a few wrong answer choices within two minutes and move on. Do not get caught up spending too much time on an Analyze Structure question.

One subtype of Analyze Structure questions has two boldface statements. Your task is to determine the role that each boldface statement plays in the argument. At the simplest level, there are three primary options for each statement:

> (1) The statement in boldface is the author's CONCLUSION.
> (2) The statement in boldface is a premise that SUPPORTS the author's conclusion.
> (3) The statement in boldface is a premise that WEAKENS the author's conclusion.

Thus, you should classify each statement according to these categories.

Consider the following example:

> Mathematician: Recently, Zubin Ghosh made headlines when he was recognized to have solved the Hilbert Conjecture, made a hundred years ago. Ghosh simply posted his work on the Internet, rather than submitting it to established journals. In fact, he has **no job, let alone a university position**; he lives alone and has refused all acclaim. In reporting on Ghosh, the press unfortunately has reinforced the popular view that mathematicians are anti-social loners. But **mathematicians actually form a tightly knit community**, frequently collaborating on important efforts; indeed, teams of researchers are working together to extend Ghosh's findings.
>
> In the argument above, the two portions in boldface play which of the following roles?
>
> (A) The first is an observation the author makes to illustrate a social pattern; the second is a generalization of that pattern.
> (B) The first is evidence in favor of the popular view expressed in the argument; the second is a brief restatement of that view.
> (C) The first is a specific example of a generalization that the author contradicts; the second is a reiteration of that generalization.
> (D) The first is a specific counterexample to a generalization that the author asserts; the second is that generalization.
> (E) The first is a detail provided in support of the primary assertion expressed in the argument; the second is that statement.

The author's conclusion is that *mathematicians actually form a tightly knit community.* The counterargument is that *mathematicians are antisocial loners.* Now, label each statement as either Conclusion, Premise For, or Premise Against. In the above argument, the first boldface represents an example that supports the counterargument. Thus, the first statement is Premise Against. The second boldface represents the author's conclusion. Now we can write down our assessment of the boldface statements:

#1 = Premise Against
#2 = Conclusion

Turning to the answer choices, we should assess each one methodically.

Evaluate the first half of choice **(A)** first. This says that the author uses this statement to illustrate a social pattern. In other words, this choice asserts that statement #1 is Premise For. We have labeled the first statement as Premise Against, so this choice is incorrect.

The first half of choice **(B)** says the first statement supports the popular view. The popular view is the counterargument, so this choice argues that #1 is Premise Against. The second half of choice **(B)**, however, says that the second statement is the popular view. The second statement is the author's conclusion, not the counterargument. Eliminate this choice.

The first half of choice **(C)** says that the first statement is an example of the counterargument (in other words, Premise Against). The second half of choice **(C)** says that the second statement reiterates the counterargument, but the second statement is the author's own conclusion. Eliminate this choice.

The first half of choice **(D)** says that the first statement is a counterexample to the author's conclusion (in other words, Premise Against). The second half of choice **(D)** says that the second statement is the author's conclusion. We agree with these labels, so this is the correct answer. As always, you should read all the answer choices, but you may be at the two-minute mark already, in which case you should select **(D)** and move on.

The first half of choice **(E)** says that the first statement is a premise in support of the author's conclusion (in other words, Premise For). However, we labeled statement #1 as Premise Against. Eliminate this choice.

As discussed earlier, Analyze the Argument Structure is a very difficult question type. If you can only figure out how to categorize one of the two boldface statements, then assess the corresponding half of the answer choices. Eliminate whatever answer choices you can, pick intelligently from among the remaining answer choices, and move on.

Some Analyze Structure questions will contain only one boldface statement. In this case, you can still use the method above. Alternatively, the argument may show dialogue between two opposing speakers, say Alice and Bob. The question may ask you to analyze how Bob responded to Alice's argument. In this case, you will need to determine what logical method Bob used to refute the Alice's argument. Possibilities include (1) contradicting a premise of Alice's, (2) introducing a premise that weakens Alice's conclusion, or (3) introducing a premise that supports Bob's own conclusion.

3. Evaluate the Conclusion

Evaluate the Conclusion questions ask you to identify information that would help you evaluate the validity of a given conclusion. For example:

> Which of the following is most likely to yield information that would help to evaluate the effectiveness of the new method?

> In order to evaluate the conclusion, the most useful information would be
>
> _____.

The argument or the question will tend to introduce some type of classic hypothesis: for example, *if* X *then* Y, or X *causes* Y. The correct answer will provide a way to test the hypothesis and determine whether X will actually lead to Y.

The wrong answers appear to address pieces of the argument, but they do not actually allow you to test the proposed causal connection between X and Y.

4. Resolve a Problem

Resolve a Problem questions ask you to solve a problem posed by a passage of premises. Occasionally, the problem itself will be posed in the question. For example:

> Which of the following would best counteract the drug's effects?

> To discourage the described counterfeiting, the best approach would be to
>
> _____.

In the first question, the argument itself might not actually mention the problem, but the question indicates that you must find a way to counteract the drug's effects. In the second question, the counterfeiting would be described in the argument, and your purpose is to discourage that counterfeiting.

The correct answer should directly counteract or fix the given problem. You will not have to make additional assumptions to apply the resolution. Furthermore, the correct answer will tend to appear as a new premise.

Incorrect answers on Resolve a Problem questions tend to appear in one of two forms. Most commonly, wrong answers will appear to address some piece of the argument but will not actually counteract or fix the problem. Wrong answers may also be the result of "Wrong Direction" thinking. In these cases, the answers will range from merely reinforcing the idea that the problem exists to actually making the problem worse.

Pay attention to the specific question you are asked. Make sure that the choice you select actually answers that question.

5. Provide an Example

Provide an Example questions ask you to select a situation that best exemplifies the main point—the conclusion—of a given argument. For example:

> Which of the following illustrates the process described above?

To solve these types of questions, identify the general principle described in the argument. Look for an answer choice that describes an example from which you could deduce the principle itself.

6. Restate the Conclusion

Restate the Conclusion questions ask you to identify the main point—the conclusion—of the argument.

> Which of the following statements best summarizes the main point of the argument above?

To solve these types of questions, use your diagram to locate the conclusion and choose the answer choice that best restates or paraphrases it. Do not add in any outside thinking or make any assumptions.

7. Mimic the Argument

Mimic the Argument questions ask you to analyze the logical flow of an argument and then choose the answer choice that most closely mimics this argument flow or structure. Mimic the Argument questions are both rare and time-consuming; be sure not to spend more than two minutes on a problem of this type. If necessary, eliminate what answer choices you can in two minutes, pick intelligently from among the remaining answer choices, and move on.

> Which of the following arguments has a line of reasoning most similar to that in the argument above?

To solve these types of questions, use your diagram to identify the logical structure of the argument, including the order in which the premises and conclusion appear. Choose the answer choice that reflects the same structure and order, including any cause-effect relationships or similar logical interactions. If, in the original argument, X leads to Y and Y leads to Z, the correct answer should reflect that A leads to B and B leads to C. If, in the original argument, X does not lead to Y but instead leads to Z, the correct answer should reflect that A does not lead to B but instead leads to C. Both the original argument and the correct answer will illustrate the same overall message or "moral of the story." The specific details of the original argument will be irrelevant. Only the structure of the original argument matters.

Problem Set

The following questions are a representative sampling of various minor question types. First, try to identify the underlying problem type. Then use the strategies laid out in this chapter to solve the problem. Be sure to diagram each argument. Detailed answers and explanations follow.

1. Nitrogen Triiodide

Nitrogen triiodide is a highly explosive chemical that is easy to make from only two ingredients: ammonia and concentrated iodine. However, no terrorists are known to have ever used nitrogen triiodide in an attack.

Which of the following, if true, is the most likely explanation for the discrepancy described above?

(A) Ammonia can be bought in a grocery store, but concentrated iodine must be obtained from somewhat more restricted sources, such as chemical supply houses.
(B) Nitrogen triiodide is only one of several powerful explosives that can be made from ammonia.
(C) Many terrorists have been more focused on acquiring weapons of mass destruction, such as nuclear or biological weapons, than on developing conventional chemical explosives.
(D) Airport security devices are typically calibrated to detect nitrogen compounds, such as ammonia and ammonium compounds.
(E) Nitrogen triiodide is extremely shock sensitive and can detonate as a result of even slight movement.

2. CarStore

With information readily available on the Internet, consumers now often enter the automobile retail environment with certain models and detailed specifications in mind. In response to this trend, CarStore has decided to move toward a less aggressive sales approach. Despite the fact that members of its sales personnel have an average of ten years of experience each, CarStore has implemented a mandatory training program for all sales personnel, because

_____.

(A) the sales personnel in CarStore have historically specialized in aggressively selling automobiles and add-on features
(B) the sales personnel in CarStore do not themselves use the Internet often for their own purposes
(C) CarStore has found that most consumers do not mind negotiating over price
(D) information found on the Internet often does not reflect sales promotions at individual retail locations
(E) several retailers that compete directly with CarStore have adopted "customer-centered" sales approaches

3. Costmart Warehouse

Editorial: In order to preserve the health of its local economy, Metropolis should not permit a Costmart warehouse department store to open within city limits. It has been demonstrated that when Costmart opens a warehouse department store within a city, the bankruptcy rate of local retailers increases in that city by twenty percent over the next several years.

Which of the following questions would be most useful for evaluating the conclusion of the editorial?

(A) Does the bankruptcy rate of local retailers in a city generally stabilize several years after a Costmart warehouse department store opens?
(B) Do most residents of Metropolis currently do almost all of their shopping at stores within the city limits of Metropolis?
(C) Have other cities that have permitted Costmart warehouse department stores within city limits experienced any economic benefits as a result?
(D) Is the bankruptcy rate for local retailers in Metropolis higher than in the average city that has permitted a Costmart warehouse department store within city limits?
(E) Does Costmart plan to hire employees exclusively from within Metropolis for the proposed warehouse department store?

4. Spreading the Flu

Scientists recently documented that influenza spreads around the world more efficiently in the modern era due to commercial air travel. Symptoms of a pandemic-level flu are severe enough that the ill would likely cancel or reschedule air travel, but an infected person can travel across the globe before the first signs appear. Further, if symptoms develop while someone is still on a plane, the infected person's cough can spread the virus easily in the enclosed and closely-packed environment.

Which of the following would best minimize the role air travel can play in the spread of influenza during a pandemic?

(A) installing air filtration systems in the planes to kill any flu virus particles flowing through the filters
(B) requiring air travelers to receive flu vaccinations far enough in advance of the trip to provide protection against the disease
(C) refusing to allow children, the elderly, or others who are especially vulnerable to flu to travel by air during a pandemic
(D) requiring all air travelers to wash their hands before boarding a plane
(E) conducting medical examinations during the boarding process to weed out passengers with flu symptoms

5. Malaria

In an attempt to explain the cause of malaria, a deadly infectious disease common in tropical areas, early European settlers in Hong Kong attributed the malady to poisonous gases supposedly emanating from low-lying swampland. Malaria, in fact, translates from the Italian as "bad air." In the 1880s, however, doctors determined that Anopheles mosquitoes were responsible for transmitting the disease to humans after observing that **the female of the species can carry a parasitic protozoan that is passed on to unsuspecting humans when a mosquito feasts on a person's blood.**

What function does the statement in **boldface** fulfill with respect to the argument presented above?

(A) It provides support for the explanation of a particular phenomenon.
(B) It presents evidence which contradicts an established fact.
(C) It offers confirmation of a contested assumption.
(D) It identifies the cause of an erroneous conclusion.
(E) It proposes a new conclusion in place of an earlier conjecture.

6. Deer Hunters

Due to the increase in traffic accidents caused by deer in the state, the governor last year reintroduced a longer deer hunting season to encourage recreational hunting of the animals. The governor expected the longer hunting season to decrease the number of deer and therefore decrease the number of accidents. However, this year the number of accidents caused by deer has increased substantially since the reintroduction of the longer deer hunting season.

Which of the following, if true, would best explain the increase in traffic accidents caused by deer?

(A) Many recreational hunters hunt only once or twice per hunting season, regardless of the length of the season.
(B) The deer in the state have become accustomed to living in close proximity to humans and are often easy prey for hunters as a result.
(C) Most automobile accidents involving deer result from cars swerving to avoid deer, and leave the deer in question unharmed.
(D) The number of drivers in the state has been gradually increasing over the past several years.
(E) A heavily used new highway was recently built directly through the state's largest forest, which is the primary habitat of the state's deer population.

7. Law of Demand

The law of demand states that, if all other factors remain equal, the higher the price of a good, the less people will consume that good. In other words, the higher the price, the lower the quantity demanded. This principle is illustrated when _____.

(A) Company A has a monopoly over the widget market so an increase in widget prices has little effect on the quantity demanded
(B) a manufacturer of luxury cars noticed that its customer base is relatively unresponsive to changes in price
(C) the recent increase in gas prices caused an increased demand for fuel-efficient cars
(D) an increase in the number of computer retailers led to a decrease in the average price of computers
(E) a reduction in the price of oranges from $2 per pound to $1 per pound results in 75 pounds of oranges being sold as opposed to 50 pounds

8. Private Equity

In past decades, private equity investors used to compete for exclusive participation in investments. Now, in response to both the growing scale of investments and increased competition to participate, private equity funds often form syndicates or "clubs" and jointly take positions in large investments. Clearly, the reason investors do this is to allow them to spread some of the risk and also gain access to a broader range of investments and opportunities.

Which of the following statements by a private equity investor best defines the changing attitude described in the argument above?

(A) "We would rather beat our competition by working with them in order to find out their strengths and weaknesses."

(B) "In order to keep up with our competition, we should stop investing small and only invest in very large opportunities."

(C) "In order to make sure that we can participate in certain investments, we should expect to cooperate with our competition on occasion."

(D) "To avoid taking any risks, it is necessary to stop competing with our former competitors."

(E) "In response to changing market conditions, we should participate only in investments that allow us to take better positions than our competitors."

9. Executive Debate

Media Critic: Network executives have alleged that television viewership is decreasing due to the availability of television programs on other platforms, such as the internet, video-on-demand, and mobile devices. These executives claim that **declining viewership will cause advertising revenue to fall so far that networks will be unable to spend the large sums necessary to produce programs of the quality now available**. That development, in turn, will lead to a dearth of programming for the very devices which cannibalized television's audience. However, technology executives point to research which indicates that **users of these platforms increase the number of hours per week that they watch television** because they are exposed to new programs and promotional spots through these alternate platforms. This analysis demonstrates that networks can actually increase their revenue through higher advertising rates, due to larger audiences lured to television through other media.

The portions in **boldface** play which of the following roles in the media critic's argument?

(A) The first is an inevitable trend that weighs against the critic's claim; the second is that claim.

(B) The first is a prediction that is challenged by the argument; the second is a finding upon which the argument depends.

(C) The first clarifies the reasoning behind the critic's claim; the second demonstrates why that claim is flawed.

(D) The first acknowledges a position that the technology executives accept as true; the second is a consequence of that position.

(E) The first opposes the critic's claim through an analogy; the second outlines a scenario in which that claim will not hold.

10. Immigration Trends

As a percentage of the total population in the United States, the foreign-born population increased from 4.7 percent in 1970 to 11.1 percent in 2000. However, given historical immigration patterns, this trend is unlikely to continue in the 21st century.

Which of the following is most like the argument above in its logical structure?

(A) The birth rate in Town T increased dramatically between 1970 and 2000. However, between 2000 and 2005, the birth rate decreased slightly.

(B) The gray wolf population in Minnesota grew nearly 50 percent between 1996 and 2005. However, during the same time period, the gray wolf population in Montana only increased by around 13 percent.

(C) Company A's sales have decreased over the past two quarters. However, as sales typically increase during the fourth quarter, Company A predicts that sales will not continue to go down.

(D) Per capita soft drink consumption in the United States has increased by nearly 500% over the past 50 years. In order to combat the affiliated health risks, some soft drink manufacturers are developing carbonated milk drinks to be sold in schools.

(E) The number of televisions sold in Country Q decreased by 20% between 2005 and 2006. However, the average number of hours spent watching television in Country Q more than doubled.

1. Nitrogen Triiodide

Nitrogen triiodide is a highly explosive chemical that is easy to make from only two ingredients: ammonia and concentrated iodine. However, no terrorists are known to have ever used nitrogen triiodide in an attack.

Which of the following, if true, is the most likely explanation for the discrepancy described above?

(A) Ammonia can be bought in a grocery store, but concentrated iodine must be obtained from somewhat more restricted sources, such as chemical supply houses.

(B) Nitrogen triiodide is only one of several powerful explosives that can be made from ammonia.

(C) Many terrorists have been more focused on acquiring weapons of mass destruction, such as nuclear or biological weapons, than on developing conventional chemical explosives.

(D) Airport security devices are typically calibrated to detect nitrogen compounds, such as ammonia and ammonium compounds.

(E) Nitrogen triiodide is extremely shock sensitive and can detonate as a result of even slight movement.

The question presents seemingly contradictory premises. On the one hand, nitrogen triiodide is a powerful explosive that is easy to make from just two ingredients. On the other hand, apparently no terrorists have used this chemical in attacks. The correct answer will reconcile these premises by presenting a relevant, reasonable explanation for why terrorists have not used this explosive, despite its advantages. Thus, the correct answer should convey a direct <u>disadvantage</u> of using the explosive.

(A) This answer choice does present an obstacle: one of the ingredients has limited availability. However, the obstacle is not described as serious. The ingredient can be obtained from *somewhat more restricted sources* than a grocery store, such *chemical supply houses.*

(B) Other explosives can be made from ammonia, but this fact does not satisfactorily explain why terrorists have not used this particular explosive.

(C) This answer choice presents another obstacle: many terrorists are more focused on weapons of mass destruction than on these kinds of chemical explosives. However, this does not mean that all terrorists are more focused on weapons of mass destruction. Moreover, even terrorists who are more focused on more devastating weapons may still be interested enough in conventional explosives to use nitrogen triiodide in some attack.

(D) Airport security devices may be calibrated to detect ammonium compounds, an obstacle to their use in attacks on planes or airports. But terrorists might still use such compounds in other sorts of attacks.

(E) CORRECT. Only this answer choice presents a clear and serious obstacle to the use of nitrogen triiodide in terrorist attacks. Since simply moving around with the chemical might cause it to detonate, terrorists are unlikely to use such an unstable chemical in attacks.

2. CarStore

With information readily available on the Internet, consumers now often enter the automobile retail environment with certain models and detailed specifications in mind. In response to this trend, CarStore has decided to move toward a less aggressive sales approach. Despite the fact that members of its sales personnel have an average of ten years of experience each, CarStore has implemented a mandatory training program for all sales personnel, because _____.

(A) the sales personnel in CarStore have historically specialized in aggressively selling automobiles and add-on features

(B) the sales personnel in CarStore do not themselves use the Internet often for their own purposes

(C) CarStore has found that most consumers do not mind negotiating over price

(D) information found on the Internet often does not reflect sales promotions at individual retail locations

(E) several retailers that compete directly with CarStore have adopted "customer-centered" sales approaches

The argument describes CarStore's decision to move toward a less aggressive sales approach in response to consumers now entering the retail environment with automobile models and specifications in mind. This is presented implicitly in contrast to how consumers entered the retail environment prior to the Internet. The passage then states that, despite the fact that its sales personnel are very experienced, CarStore is implementing a mandatory training program. We are asked to complete the passage; the explanation for the training program should resolve the apparent discrepancy between the extensive experience of CarStore's employees and the company's new mandatory training program.

(A) CORRECT. If the sales personnel at CarStore have historically specialized in aggressive sales tactics and promoting add-on features, they will need to learn new sales tactics. This explains the need for a mandatory retraining program. This answer choice also ties directly to the first and second premises provided, as aggressive selling is less appropriate if consumers already know what model and features they would like to purchase.

(B) Though it may be helpful for the sales personnel of CarStore to use the Internet themselves so that they can relate to many of their customers, this is irrelevant to the argument. The argument describes CarStore's new policy as promoting a less aggressive sales approach; there is no indication that the training should involve edifying salespeople about how to use the Internet.

(C) The fact that consumers do not mind negotiating over price, if true, suggests that a less aggressive sales approach may not be necessary. This does not fit logically with the overall argument abut CarStore adopting a new, less aggressive sales approach.

(D) The fact that information gained from the Internet may not be exhaustive or up-to-date is irrelevant to the argument, which centers on the need for training salespeople in a less aggressive sales approach. Also, experienced salespeople would presumably know about location-specific sales promotions and be able to describe them to consumers without any additional training.

(E) That several competitors to CarStore have adopted "customer-centered" sales approaches may help explain why CarStore has also decided on a less aggressive sales approach. However, the actions of CarStore's competitors are outside the scope of the argument. Also, this answer choice does not satisfactorily explain the need to retrain veteran salespeople.

3. Costmart Warehouse

Editorial: In order to preserve the health of its local economy, Metropolis should not permit a Costmart warehouse department store to open within city limits. It has been demonstrated that when Costmart opens a warehouse department store within a city, the bankruptcy rate of local retailers increases in that city by twenty percent over the next several years.

Which of the following questions would be most useful for evaluating the conclusion of the editorial?

(A) Does the bankruptcy rate of local retailers in a city generally stabilize several years after a Costmart warehouse department store opens?
(B) Do most residents of Metropolis currently do almost all of their shopping at stores within the city limits of Metropolis?
(C) Have other cities that have permitted Costmart warehouse department stores within city limits experienced any economic benefits as a result?
(D) Is the bankruptcy rate for local retailers in Metropolis higher than in the average city that has permitted a Costmart warehouse department store within city limits?
(E) Does Costmart plan to hire employees exclusively from within Metropolis for the proposed warehouse department store?

The editorial argues that a Costmart warehouse department store should not be permitted within city limits in order to preserve the health of the city's local economy. The evidence presented is that, in other cities, opening a Costmart warehouse department store has caused a twenty percent rise in the bankruptcy rate of local retailers for the next several years. In order to evaluate the conclusion, it would be helpful to determine whether opening a Costmart warehouse department store has any other impacts on the economic health of a city aside from increasing the bankruptcy rate of local stores.

(A) Knowing whether the bankruptcy rate of local retailers stabilizes after several years is not helpful in evaluating the conclusion. The increased bankruptcy rate is given in the premises. Also, this answer choice suggests only that the bankruptcy rate stops increasing after several years, not that there is any economic benefit to be achieved.

(B) Knowing whether most residents of Metropolis currently shop at stores in Metropolis is not helpful in evaluating the conclusion. This information does not impact the bankruptcy rate of local retailers. Similarly, this information does not directly affect the health of the local economy unless the proportion of residents that shop in Metropolis is expected to change.

(C) CORRECT. We are asked to evaluate an argument concerning whether a Costmart warehouse department store is negative for the local economy of Metropolis. It is presented that the bankruptcy rate of local retailers can be expected to increase. However, the argument is silent as to whether any benefits can be expected in the local economy as a result of the new Costmart store (e.g. lower prices for Metropolis consumers, more efficient retail operations). This information would be helpful in evaluating the conclusion.

(D) To evaluate the conclusion, it is not helpful to know whether the current bankruptcy rate of retailers in Metropolis is higher than that of retailers in the average city that has opened a Costmart warehouse department store. The bankruptcy rate would be expected to increase as a result of the new Costmart store regardless of whether the bankruptcy rate started at a higher or lower base than the average city.

(E) Knowing whether Costmart plans to hire exclusively from within Metropolis is not helpful in evaluating the economic effects of opening a Costmart warehouse within city limits. Whether the answer to this question is "yes" or "no," in general, it is still not clear what economic impact this may have, if any. For example, if other local retailers go out of business, the jobs created by Costmart may simply counterbalance the jobs lost, resulting in no net gain or loss.

4. Spreading the Flu

Scientists recently documented that influenza spreads around the world more efficiently in the modern era due to commercial air travel. Symptoms of a pandemic-level flu are severe enough that the ill would likely cancel or reschedule air travel, but an infected person can travel across the globe before the first signs appear. Further, if symptoms develop while someone is still on a plane, the infected person's cough can spread the virus easily in the enclosed and closely-packed environment. Which of the following would best minimize the role air travel can play in the spread of influenza during a pandemic?

(A) installing air filtration systems in the planes to kill any flu virus particles flowing through the filters
(B) requiring air travelers to receive flu vaccinations far enough in advance of the trip to provide protection against the disease
(C) refusing to allow children, the elderly, or others who are especially vulnerable to flu to travel by air during a pandemic
(D) requiring all air travelers to wash their hands before boarding a plane
(E) conducting medical examinations during the boarding process to weed out passengers with flu symptoms

We are presented with a paragraph of premises and asked to resolve the problem they present: how to minimize the spread of flu via air travel. The correct answer will need to rely specifically on the premises and will not require us to make any inferences or assumptions.

(A) The passage states that the infection can be spread by coughing. The flu virus, therefore, can reach the other passengers *in the closely-packed environment* before it enters any filters that might kill the virus.

(B) CORRECT. Vaccines provide significant protection against developing the virus (not 100% protection, but we are asked to *minimize* the impact of air travel, not eliminate it entirely). If all passengers are vaccinated against the virus, many of those who otherwise would have developed the disease will not, and, therefore, will not spread it to others.

(C) Anyone can contract the virus and subsequently spread it; the mentioned populations are merely *especially vulnerable* to it. Infected people traveling to another place can infect children, senior citizens and others who have stayed in their home regions.

(D) The passage states that the infection can be spread by coughing; while it may be true that the virus can also spread via hand contact, this information is not stated in the passage.

(E) The passage states that people who develop symptoms before travel begins likely would not make the trip; weeding out those with observable symptoms, then, will not *minimize* the role of air travel because most of those people will decide themselves not to take the trip. The larger danger is those who may be infected but have not yet developed symptoms.

5. Malaria

In an attempt to explain the cause of malaria, a deadly infectious disease common in tropical areas, early European settlers in Hong Kong attributed the malady to poisonous gases supposedly emanating from low-lying swampland. Malaria, in fact, translates from the Italian as "bad air." In the 1880s, however, doctors determined that Anopheles mosquitoes were responsible for transmitting the disease to humans after observing that **the female of the species can carry a parasitic protozoan that is passed on to unsuspecting humans when a mosquito feasts on a person's blood.**

What function does the statement in **boldface** fulfill with respect to the argument presented above?

(A) It provides support for the explanation of a particular phenomenon.
(B) It presents evidence which contradicts an established fact.
(C) It offers confirmation of a contested assumption.
(D) It identifies the cause of an erroneous conclusion.
(E) It proposes a new conclusion in place of an earlier conjecture.

This problem is an Analyze the Argument Structure question. The first step is to identify the conclusion of the argument, which appears in the third sentence: *Doctors determined that Anopheles mosquitoes were responsible for transmitting the disease to humans.* The boldface statement provides the specific mechanism by which the mosquito is responsible for human infection; it therefore supports the ultimate conclusion. More simply, the boldface represents a Premise For.

(A) CORRECT. The statement is a supporting premise which explains why the conclusion is true.

(B) The statement does provide evidence which contradicts the original belief, but the original belief cannot be labeled a fact; it was a mistaken belief. If we assume that the "established fact" is the later conclusion by the doctors, then the statement does not contradict that conclusion.

(C) The statement does confirm the doctors' conclusion, but the doctors' conclusion was never contested, or in doubt. Rather, the doctors' conclusion had the effect of casting doubt on the original mistaken belief.

(D) The statement does not identify the cause of an erroneous, or mistaken, conclusion; rather, it supports a valid conclusion.

(E) The statement is not the actual conclusion; it is a premise in support of the doctors' conclusion.

6. Deer Hunters

Due to the increase in traffic accidents caused by deer in the state, the governor last year reintroduced a longer deer hunting season to encourage recreational hunting of the animals. The governor expected the longer hunting season to decrease the number of deer and therefore decrease the number of accidents. However, this year the number of accidents caused by deer has increased substantially since the reintroduction of the longer deer hunting season.

Which of the following, if true, would best explain the increase in traffic accidents caused by deer?

(A) Many recreational hunters hunt only once or twice per hunting season, regardless of the length of the season.
(B) The deer in the state have become accustomed to living in close proximity to humans and are often easy prey for hunters as a result.
(C) Most automobile accidents involving deer result from cars swerving to avoid deer, and leave the deer in question unharmed.
(D) The number of drivers in the state has been gradually increasing over the past several years.
(E) A heavily used new highway was recently built directly through the state's largest forest, which is the primary habitat of the state's deer population.

The passage states that the governor of a state is trying to resolve a problem that is apparently created by an overpopulation of deer in the state. To resolve this problem, the governor extended the recreational hunting season. However, since the reintroduction of the longer hunting season, the number of accidents caused by deer has not declined—it has in fact substantially increased. We are asked to resolve this contradiction.

(A) The fact that many hunters only hunt once or twice per hunting season regardless of the length of the season may help to explain the inefficacy of the governor's measure. However, this would not explain the observed *increase* in accidents.

(B) This answer choice, if anything, indicates that the governor's extension of the hunting season would be effective in reducing the deer overpopulation. It does not explain the increase in traffic accidents.

(C) The fact that deer often are left unharmed by traffic accidents does not explain any increase in accidents. Unless one assumes that the deer population is growing dramatically, this information suggests a constant rate of accidents.

(D) This answer choice would contribute to an explanation of a gradual increase in traffic accidents involving deer over the last several years. However, it does not explain a *substantial* increase in accidents from last year to this year. Both the extent of the increase and the time frame serve to make this answer choice an unsatisfactory explanation of the observed rise in accidents.

(E) CORRECT. A new highway system recently built directly through the primary habitat of the state's deer population would provide a specific explanation as to why the number of accidents involving deer has increased. It also explains the time frame of the increase.

7. Law of Demand

The law of demand states that, if all other factors remain equal, the higher the price of a good, the less people will consume that good. In other words, the higher the price, the lower the quantity demanded. This principle is illustrated when _____.

(A) Company A has a monopoly over the widget market so an increase in widget prices has little effect on the quantity demanded
(B) a manufacturer of luxury cars noticed that its customer base is relatively unresponsive to changes in price
(C) the recent increase in gas prices caused an increased demand for fuel-efficient cars
(D) an increase in the number of computer retailers led to a decrease in the average price of computers
(E) a reduction in the price of oranges from $2 per pound to $1 per pound results in 75 pounds of oranges being sold as opposed to 50 pounds

The passage describes the law of demand, which states that the higher the price, the lower the quantity demanded. Alternatively, the law could be restated as indicating that the lower the price, the greater the quantity demanded.

(A) An increase in the price of widgets does not decrease the quantity demanded. This does not illustrate the principle described in the argument.

(B) Changes in the price of luxury cars do not have an effect on the quantity demanded. This does not illustrate the principle described in the argument.

(C) This example discusses the effect of the price of a related item, gas, on the quantity of fuel-efficient cars demanded. It does not directly illustrate the law of demand for a particular good as determined by its price.

(D) This example describes the effect of increased availability or competition and a decrease in price. It does not directly illustrate a relationship between price and demand.

(E) CORRECT. This example demonstrates the principle of the law of demand: as the price of oranges decreases, the quantity demanded increases.

8. *Private Equity*

In past decades, private equity investors used to compete for exclusive participation in investments. Now, in response to both the growing scale of investments and increased competition to participate, private equity funds often form syndicates or "clubs" and jointly take positions in large investments. Clearly, the reason investors do this is to allow them to spread some of the risk and also gain access to a broader range of investments and opportunities.

Which of the following statements by a private equity investor best defines the changing attitude described in the argument above?

(A) "We would rather beat our competition by working with them in order to find out their strengths and weaknesses."
(B) "In order to keep up with our competition, we should stop investing small and only invest in very large opportunities."
(C) "In order to make sure that we can participate in certain investments, we should expect to cooperate with our competition on occasion."
(D) "To avoid taking any risks, it is necessary to stop competing with our former competitors."
(E) "In response to changing market conditions, we should participate only in investments that allow us to take better positions than our competitors."

The argument describes private equity investors as very competitive with one another in past decades. However, the argument indicates that this has changed in response to changing market conditions. Specifically, as investments have become larger in scale and competition to participate in investments has increased, private equity funds have begun to cooperate with one another and pool resources in large investments. The author concludes that investors do this to gain two advantages: the sharing of risk and the ability to gain access to a broader range of investments and opportunities. We are asked to choose a quote that best reflects this conclusion.

(A) The argument does not include any reference to determining the strengths and weaknesses of one's competitors. Also, there is no indication that this cooperative approach allows investors to *beat*, or obtain better results than, their competitors.

(B) The argument does refer to increased competition as one catalyst for the change in approach. However, there is no indication in the argument that private equity investors now *only* invest in very large opportunities. Rather, the argument states that investments have become larger in scale, requiring cooperation among investors.

(C) CORRECT. The increasing scale of investments and increased competition are cited as pressures that encourage cooperation among private equity investors in order to ensure participation in certain investments. Also, the second part of this answer choice accurately characterizes the argument's description of the attitude toward competition that has been adopted by private equity investors.

*Manhattan*GMAT*Prep
the new standard

(D) While the argument does state that the ability to spread risk is a benefit of cooperation, the phrase *to avoid taking any risks* is inaccurate and too extreme. Also, the argument does not indicate that it is necessary to stop competing; cooperating with competitors in certain instances is not the same as not competing.

(E) The argument does mention changing market conditions. However, the argument does not indicate that cooperation in a joint investment is contingent upon taking a more advantaged position than one's competitors. Indeed, it would be impossible for <u>all</u> investors to invest only when they have an advantage relative to the other investors.

9. Executive Debate

Media Critic: Network executives have alleged that television viewership is decreasing due to the availability of television programs on other platforms, such as the internet, video-on-demand, and mobile devices. These executives claim that **declining viewership will cause advertising revenue to fall so far that networks will be unable to spend the large sums necessary to produce programs of the quality now available.** That development, in turn, will lead to a dearth of programming for the very devices which cannibalized television's audience. However, technology executives point to research which indicates that **users of these platforms increase the number of hours per week that they watch television** because they are exposed to new programs and promotional spots through these alternate platforms. This analysis demonstrates that networks can actually increase their revenue through higher advertising rates, due to larger audiences lured to television through other media.

The portions in **boldface** play which of the following roles in the media critic's argument?

(A) The first is an inevitable trend that weighs against the critic's claim; the second is that claim.

(B) The first is a prediction that is challenged by the argument; the second is a finding upon which the argument depends.

(C) The first clarifies the reasoning behind the critic's claim; the second demonstrates why that claim is flawed.

(D) The first acknowledges a position that the technology executives accept as true; the second is a consequence of that position.

(E) The first opposes the critic's claim through an analogy; the second outlines a scenario in which that claim will not hold.

This problem is an Analyze the Argument Structure question. In order to properly evaluate the role of the two boldface portions, we must first identify the critic's conclusion: *Networks can actually increase their revenue through higher advertising rates, due to larger audiences lured to television through other media.* The first boldface portion opposes this position by predicting smaller audiences; the second lends support to it by citing evidence that alternate media platforms lead their users to watch more television. More simply, the first boldface statement is a Premise Against, and the second boldface statement is a Premise For. The correct answer choice will reflect this pattern.

(A) The first boldface statement does weigh against the critic's claim, but it is a prediction, rather than *an inevitable trend*. The second boldface statement supports the claim; it is not the conclusion itself.

(B) CORRECT. The critic's conclusion about a potential increase in network revenue is contrary to the first boldface statement's prediction about shrinking audiences and falling revenue. Also, the argument in fact depends upon the second boldface statement's assertion that users of alternate devices will actually watch more hours of television.

(C) The first boldface statement opposes the critic's claim, rather than clarifies it. The second boldface statement is used to support the critic's claim; it does not indicate that the critic's claim is flawed.

(D) The description of the first boldface statement is incorrect in that the technology executives neither accept nor deny the prediction of the network executives. The second boldface statement contradicts, rather than follows as a consequence of, that prediction.

(E) The first boldface statement is incorrect described, because it does not use an analogy. The second boldface statement is in agreement with, not in opposition to, the critic's claim.

10. *Immigration Trends*

As a percentage of the total population in the United States, the foreign-born population increased from 4.7 percent in 1970 to 11.1 percent in 2000. However, given historical immigration patterns, this trend is unlikely to continue in the 21st century.

Which of the following is most like the argument above in its logical structure?

(A) The birth rate in Town T increased dramatically between 1970 and 2000. However, between 2000 and 2005, the birth rate decreased slightly.
(B) The gray wolf population in Minnesota grew nearly 50 percent between 1996 and 2005. However, during the same time period, the gray wolf population in Montana only increased by around 13 percent.
(C) Company A's sales have decreased over the past two quarters. However, as sales typically increase during the fourth quarter, Company A predicts that sales will not continue to go down.
(D) Per capita soft drink consumption in the United States has increased by nearly 500% over the past 50 years. In order to combat the affiliated health risks, some soft drink manufacturers are developing carbonated milk drinks to be sold in schools.
(E) The number of televisions sold in Country Q decreased by 20% between 2005 and 2006. However, the average number of hours spent watching television in Country Q more than doubled.

The original argument states that although the foreign-born population increased from 1970 to 2000, historical data indicates that this trend is unlikely to continue into the 21st century. The argument first states a trend that has been observed in the past. The argument then concludes that, given other historical information, this trend will likely not continue in the future.

(A) This argument states a trend that has been observed in the past: the birth rate for Town T increased between 1970 and 2000. The argument then states a different trend that has been observed in the past: the birth rate decreased slightly between 2000 and 2005. There is no prediction of a different result in the future; this answer choice does not mimic the original argument.

(B) This argument is a comparison of two trends over the same period of time: The wolf population in Minnesota increased more dramatically than that in Montana. There is no prediction of
a different result in the future; this answer choice does not mimic the original argument.

(C) CORRECT. This argument states a trend and then concludes that this trend will not continue
in the future, given other historical information. Company A's sales have decreased in the past,
but the argument predicts that sales will not continue to go down because of historical sales
data related to the fourth quarters of previous years.

(D) This argument states a trend and then a fact related to this trend. Per capita soft drink consumption in the United States has increased and as a result, some soft drink manufacturers are
developing carbonated milk drinks. There is no prediction of a different result in the future;
this answer choice does not mimic the original argument.

(E) This argument lists two contrasting trends: the number of televisions decreased, but the average
number of hours spent watching television increased. There is no prediction of a different result
in the future; this answer choice does not mimic the original argument.

REAL GMAT PROBLEMS

Now that you have completed your study of MINOR QUESTION TYPES, it is time to test your skills on passages that have appeared on real GMAT exams over the past several years.

The problem set below is composed of Critical Reasoning passages from two books published by GMAC (Graduate Management Admission Council):

The Official Guide for GMAT Review, 11th Edition (pages 32–38 & 468–504)
The Official Guide for GMAT Verbal Review (pages 116–142)

Diagram each argument and answer each question.

<u>Note</u>: Problem numbers preceded by "D" refer to questions in the Diagnostic Test chapter of *The Official Guide for GMAT Review, 11th Edition* (pages 32–38).

Explain an Event or Discrepancy
> *11th Edition:* 4, 11, 22, 45, 49, 74, 82, 99, 119, D19, D33
> *Verbal Review:* 9, 23, 61, 62, 66, 72, 73

Analyze the Argument Structure
> *11th Edition:* 87, 90, 94
> *Verbal Review:* 78, 82

Evaluate the Conclusion
> *11th Edition:* 24, 106, 108, D21, D22, D29
> *Verbal Review:* 41, 65

Resolve a Problem
> *11th Edition:* 8, 58
> *Verbal Review:* 10, 30

Provide an Example
> *Verbal Review:* 5, 38

Restate the Conclusion
> *Verbal Review:* 42

Mimic the Argument
> *Verbal Review:* 8

To waive "Finance I" at Harvard Business School you must:
    (A) Be a CFA
    (B) Have prior coursework in finance
    (C) Have two years of relevant work experience in the financial sector
    (D) Pass a waiver exam
    (E) None of the above; one cannot waive core courses at HBS

What are the requirements of an Entrepreneurial Management major at the Wharton School?
    (1) Completion of 5 credit units (cu) that qualify for the major
    (2) Participation in the Wharton Business Plan Competition during the 2nd year of the MBA program

(A) Statement (1) ALONE is sufficient, but statement (2) alone is not sufficient.
(B) Statement (2) ALONE is sufficient, but statement (1) alone is not sufficient.
(C) BOTH statements TOGETHER are sufficient, but NEITHER statement ALONE is sufficient.
(D) EACH statement ALONE is sufficient.
(E) Statements (1) and (2) TOGETHER are NOT sufficient.

Once You Ace the GMAT, Get Ready to Ace Your Applications!

To make an informed decision in applying to a school—and to craft an effective application that demonstrates an appreciation of a program's unique merits—**it's crucial that you do your homework.** Clear Admit School Guides cut through the gloss of marketing materials to give you the hard facts about a program, and then put these school-specific details in context so you can see how programs compare. In the guides, you'll find detailed, comparative information on vital topics such as:

- The core curriculum and first-year experience
- Leading professors in key fields
- Student clubs and conferences
- Full-time job placement by industry and location
- Student demographics
- International and experiential learning programs
- Tuition, financial aid and scholarships
- Admissions deadlines and procedures

Now available for top schools including:
Chicago, Columbia, Harvard, Kellogg, MIT, Stanford, Tuck and Wharton

A time-saving source of comprehensive information, Clear Admit School Guides have been featured in *The Economist* and lauded by applicants, business school students and MBA graduates:

"**Purchasing the Clear Admit HBS School Guide was one of best decisions I made. I** visited HBS three times and have every book and pamphlet that covers the top business schools, but nothing can compare to the Clear Admit guides in offering up-to-date information on every aspect of the school's academic and social life that is not readily available on the school's website and brochures. Reading a Clear Admit School Guide gives an applicant the necessary, detailed school information to be competitive in the application process."
—An applicant to Harvard

CLEAR ADMIT
School Guides

"I want to tip my hat to the team at Clear Admit that put these guides together. I'm a recent graduate of Wharton's MBA program and remain active in the admissions process (serving as an alumni interviewer to evaluate applicants). I can't tell you how important it is for applicants to show genuine enthusiasm for Wharton and I think the Clear Admit School Guide for Wharton captures many of the important details, as well as the spirit of the school. **This sort of information is a must for the serious MBA applicant.**"
—A Wharton MBA graduate

Question #1: (e) and Question #2 (a)

www.clearadmit.com/schoolguides

contact us at mbaguides@clearadmit.com